Banking and Finance
Sector-Specific Plan

An Annex to the National Infrastructure Protection Plan

2010

 Homeland Security

 U.S. Department of the Treasury

Preface

November 5, 2012

We are writing to transmit the Banking and Finance Sector-Specific Plan (SSP), which was prepared and approved in 2010. The U.S. Department of the Treasury, as the Sector-Specific Agency for the Banking and Finance Sector, developed this SSP through close collaboration with the members of the Financial and Banking Information Infrastructure Committee (FBIIC) and with the private sector members of the Financial Services Sector Coordinating Council for Critical Infrastructure Protection and Homeland Security (FSSCC). Collectively, input was received from over 100 organizations representing all aspects of the sector.

The Banking and Finance Sector is large in both the number of assets and the number of individual businesses. For example, the sector includes: more than 18,800 federally insured depository institutions; thousands of providers of various investment products, including roughly 18,440 broker-dealer, investment advisers, and investment company complexes; providers of risk transfer products, including 7,948 domestic U.S. insurers; and many thousands of other credit and financing organizations. Collectively, these organizations form the backbone of the Nation's economy and a vital component of the global economy. They are tied together through a network of electronic systems with innumerable entry points. A successful attack on these systems would have detrimental effects on the entire economy. To help manage this risk, the Department of the Treasury and its government and private sector partners have developed this Banking and Finance SSP.

The Banking and Finance SSP provides the unifying structure for the integration of sector protection efforts into a single national program to help achieve the goal of a safe, secure, and resilient America through enhanced protection of the Nation's critical infrastructure and key resources (CIKR). As an annex to the National Infrastructure Protection Plan (NIPP), the Banking and Finance SSP describes how the NIPP risk management framework is being implemented in and integrated across the Banking and Finance Sector.

This release of the 2010 Banking and Finance SSP reflects the maturation of the sector partnership and the progress of the sector programs first outlined in the 2007 SSP. Examples of Banking and Finance Sector accomplishments since publication of the 2007 SSP include:

- Conducting regular testing of the FBIIC emergency communications systems.
- Identifying and assessing dependencies on other sectors, including Communications, Energy, Information Technology, and Transportation Systems.
- Sponsoring, organizing, and encouraging participation in outreach meetings for financial services representatives across the country regarding infrastructure protection issues, including how the FBIIC and the private sector operate as national partnerships, and how regional coalitions are an important part of the national strategy.
- Expanding the membership and activities of the regional coalitions.
- Promulgating new regulations to ensure resilience and redundancy.

Each year, the Banking and Finance Sector CIKR Protection Annual Report provides updates on the sector's efforts to identify, prioritize, and coordinate the protection of its critical infrastructure. The Sector Annual Report presents the current priorities of the sector as well as the progress made during the past year in following the plans and strategies set out in the Banking and Finance SSP.

This SSP represents a collaborative effort between the private sector, federal regulatory agencies, the Treasury Department, and State financial regulators. This collaboration will result in the prioritization of protection initiatives and investments within and across sectors to ensure that resources can be applied where they contribute the most to risk mitigation by lowering vulnerabilities, deterring threats, and minimizing the consequences of attacks and other incidents.

The Banking and Finance Government Coordinating Council and Sector Coordinating Council (FBIIC and FSSCC) are pleased to support this SSP and look forward to sustaining and enhancing the protection and resilience of critical infrastructure in the Banking and Finance Sector.

Leigh Williams

Banking & Finance Government
Coordinating Council/ Financial and Banking
Information Infrastructure Committee
U.S. Department of the Treasury

Todd M. Keil

Assistant Secretary for Infrastructure Protection
U.S. Department of Homeland Security

Charles Blauner

Chair
Financial Services Sector Coordinating Council

James M. Wells, III

Vice Chair
Financial Services Sector Coordinating Council

Table of Contents

Executive Summary

The Banking and Finance Sector represents a vital component of our critical national infrastructure. Large-scale power outages, recent natural disasters, and an increase in the number and sophistication of cyber attacks demonstrate the wide range of potential risks facing the sector. With this understanding, financial regulators and the financial sector work collaboratively to achieve a high degree of resilience in the face of a myriad of potential disasters, be they intentional or unintentional, manmade or natural.

Working through this public-private partnership, the U.S. Department of the Treasury (Treasury Department), as the Sector-Specific Agency (SSA) for the Banking and Finance Sector, updated this Sector-Specific Plan (SSP) in collaboration with the Financial and Banking Information Infrastructure Committee (FBIIC) and the financial services sector. This updated SSP, along with the SSPs from the other 17 critical infrastructure sectors identified in Homeland Security Presidential Directive 7 (HSPD-7) or subsequently, is part of the overall National Infrastructure Protection Plan (NIPP). This SSP contains the strategy for working collaboratively with public and private partners to identify, prioritize, and coordinate critical infrastructure resilience efforts.

Sector Profile and Goals

The Banking and Finance SSP provides a description of the complex nature of the sector and an overview of the sector's provision of products and services, which are: 1) deposit, consumer credit, and payment systems; 2) credit and liquidity products; 3) investment products; and 4) risk transfer products (including insurance).

Essential to this sector overview is the description of the Federal and State regulatory authorities as well as self-regulatory organizations. The Banking and Finance Sector is highly regulated by authorities that provide oversight and, in some cases, guidance to and examinations of the financial institutions within their statutory purview. The financial regulators work together through the FBIIC to coordinate efforts with respect to critical infrastructure resilience issues. The FBIIC was established in October 2001. It is chartered under the President's Working Group on Financial Markets and is formally chaired by the Treasury Department's Assistant Secretary for Financial Institutions.

The private sector component of the resilience partnership is organized through various organizations, such as the Financial Services Coordinating Council for Infrastructure Protection and Homeland Security (FSSCC), the Financial Services Information Sharing and Analysis Center (FS-ISAC), and the regional coalitions. These organizations promote security and resilience of the sector and voluntary information sharing. The FS-ISAC shares specific information pertaining to physical and cyber threats, vulnerabilities, incidents, and potential protective measures and practices. The regional coalitions build relationships and share information among financial institutions and first responders, emergency management personnel, and officials at the local level.

The public sector members share the following vision statement:

Vision Statement

To continue to improve the resilience and availability of financial services, the Banking and Finance Sector will work through its public-private partnership to address the evolving nature of threats and the risks posed by the sector's dependency upon other critical sectors.

To meet this vision, the Banking and Finance Sector has three primary goals:

1) To achieve the best possible position in the face of a myriad of intentional, unintentional, manmade, and natural threats against the sector's physical and cyber infrastructure;

2) To address and manage the risks posed by the dependence of the sector on the Communications, Information Technology (IT), Energy, and Transportation Systems Sectors; and

3) To work with the law enforcement community, financial regulatory authorities, the private sector, and our international counterparts to address threats facing the financial services sector.

Identifying Assets, Systems, and Networks

The products offered by the Banking and Finance Sector are largely intangible. Thus, efforts to identify assets are largely focused on critical processes rather than physical assets. The FBIIC agencies, through their oversight authority, obtain vast amounts of information on institutions, critical assets, and processes. The data that is collected is part of the regulatory process, but also serves as the basis for identifying critical infrastructure. This data is verified and updated through the continual process of regulatory examinations and mandated reporting.

Assess Risks

Risk assessments are a long-standing and accepted practice within the Banking and Finance Sector by both the regulators and the private sector. The Treasury Department and the FBIIC agencies meet regularly with financial institutions to determine whether any new assets or processes may be critical to the operations of the sector and, thus, require special attention regarding evolving threats and potential vulnerabilities.

The Banking and Finance Sector assesses consequences based on whether the loss or impairment of an asset or process would impact the sector's ability to operate in an orderly and efficient manner. The sector participants also consider the potential impact on the public's confidence in the financial system as a whole. Through vulnerability assessments, the Banking and Finance Sector has determined that some of its greatest challenges are its dependence on the Communications, Energy, IT, and Transportation Systems Sectors. Threat assessments are conducted by the sector in collaboration with other members of the intelligence, national security, and homeland security communities.

Prioritize Infrastructure

The Treasury Department, in conjunction with the FBIIC agencies and the private sector, identifies and prioritizes key infrastructure. This prioritization is based on an assessment of the impact on the orderly and efficient operation of the sector and the impact on public confidence if the specific infrastructure was no longer able to operate or was to be impaired. Factors underlying the assessment for prioritization include: the degree of dependence on the asset; the presence or absence of alternatives to the infrastructure; the public need for the services provided by the asset; the potential impact of disruption to the financial system; and the potential impacts on the economy resulting from a cascading disruption of other critical infrastructure and key resources (CIKR).

Develop and Implement Protective Programs and Resilience Strategies

Both the public and private sectors have key roles to play in implementing protective programs and resilience strategies. Through direct mandates and regulatory authority, financial regulators have specific regulatory tools that they may implement in response to a crisis. Additionally, many of the FBIIC agencies have developed and begun implementing numerous protective programs to meet the stated security and resilience goals. These protective programs range from developing and testing robust emergency communication protocols to conducting and participating in a variety of resilience efforts.

Measure Effectiveness

The Treasury Department worked with public and private sector partners to update sector-specific metrics to align them with the sector goals. The process for developing these metrics incorporates collaboration with and insights from sector participants and regulators as well as other sectors' Government and Sector Coordinating Councils, as appropriate. The FBIIC continually evaluates its protective programs for efficiency. The evaluations serve as the basis for further regulations and guidance.

Due to its complexity, measurements of the resilience efforts in the Banking and Finance Sector are difficult to quantify using standard business measurements. Therefore, a one-size-fits-all approach would be inapplicable to all aspects of the sector, and would also weaken creativity and vitality in the sector, which would harm the nation's economy overall.

CIKR Protection Research and Development

In 2006, the FSSCC formed a Research and Development (R&D) committee to develop plans and programs that would provide the most benefit to the specific CIKR requirements of the financial services sector. The FSSCC R&D committee is organized to support R&D initiatives to ensure the protection and resilience of the physical and electronic infrastructure of the Banking and Finance Sector's activities that are vital to the nation's economic well-being. The committee provides guidance for the creation of an FSSCC R&D agenda to identify and prioritize areas of need.

Managing and Coordinating SSA Responsibilities

The Assistant Secretary for Financial Institutions (ASFI) is the Treasury Department official with responsibility for carrying out the Treasury Department's duties as the SSA for the Banking and Finance Sector. As the SSA, the ASFI oversees the tri-annual rewrite of the SSP. Because the majority of the sector is privately owned, the SSA acts as an intermediary between various private entities. In this role, the SSA encourages the formation of and participation in regional councils and provides training and education.

Introduction

The U.S. Department of the Treasury (the "Treasury Department"), as the Sector-Specific Agency (SSA) for the Banking and Finance Sector, developed a Sector-Specific Plan (SSP) for critical infrastructure protection and resilience. This update to the 2007 SSP provides the Banking and Finance Sector's strategy for working collaboratively with public and private sector partners to identify, prioritize, and coordinate the protection and resilience of critical infrastructure.

1. Sector Profile and Goals

The Banking and Finance Sector infrastructure is a vital component of our critical national infrastructure. Descriptions of the sector's profile and goals necessarily include the diversity of its institutions and the services they provide. Most important to this profile is the understanding that the financial services sector is extensively regulated by Federal and, in many cases, State government. In addition to these public sector entities, self-regulatory organizations (SROs), such as the Municipal Securities Rulemaking Board (MSRB), the Financial Industry Regulatory Authority (FINRA), and the National Futures Association (NFA), also play an important role in industry oversight, as do exchanges, such as the Chicago Mercantile Exchange (CME), and designated futures exchanges.

Product diversity enables the sector as a whole to meet the needs of its large and diverse customer base. From the largest institutions with assets greater than one trillion dollars to the smallest community banks and credit unions, financial institutions provide a broad array of products. Whether it is an individual savings account, financial derivatives, credit extended to a large corporation, or investments made by a foreign country, these products: (1) allow customers to deposit funds and make payments to other parties; (2) provide credit and liquidity to customers; (3) allow customers to invest funds for both long and short periods; and (4) transfer financial risks between customers.

The diversity does not detract from the unifying mission of the U.S. financial sector to ensure its continued efficiency and the continuity of its institutions. Through the extensive regulatory regime and formalized information-sharing organizations detailed in this plan, the sector pursues wide-ranging critical infrastructure protection efforts to address security and resilience. The U.S. financial regulatory system includes both Federal and State regulatory agencies, and in some cases, SROs. Among their many responsibilities, they are concerned with institutional and systemic ability to withstand operational disruptions. Through numerous laws enacted by Congress over the past 150 years, Federal financial regulators have implemented a complex regime that in many instances provides for examinations of institutions' operational, financial, and technological systems. These examinations are designed to determine the extent to which the institution has identified its risks, including operational risks, and to evaluate the adequacy of controls and applicable risk management practices at the institution. Various non-Federal regulators may exercise similar authority.

Additionally, financial regulators update guidance to financial institutions regularly. This guidance assists the sector in staying abreast of the evolving nature of risks. Guidance on operational risks addresses means for increasing risk management and resilience in the face of potential impacts that may result from a terrorist attack, natural disaster, or other incident. These regulators have identified certain critical operational vulnerabilities, including vulnerabilities stemming from information technology (IT). (See appendix B for a list of relevant statutory authorities and examples of regulators' examination tools and guidance.)

Homeland Security Presidential Directive 7 (HSPD-7) has among its primary objectives the designation of SSAs to lead collaborative efforts for the critical infrastructure. The Treasury Department is the SSA for the Banking and Finance Sector. As the SSA, the Treasury Department works with all relevant Federal departments and agencies; State, local, and tribal governments;

and the private sector, including key persons and entities in the financial services sector, to promote efforts to improve the sector's ability to prepare for, respond to, prevent, and mitigate manmade threats, natural disasters, and other intentional or unintentional risks.

The Treasury Assistant Secretary for Financial Institutions implements the Treasury Department's responsibilities under HSPD-7. As part of fulfilling these responsibilities, the Assistant Secretary chairs the Financial and Banking Information Infrastructure Committee (FBIIC). The FBIIC is the working group comprised of the Federal financial regulators, and associations of State financial regulators. Through the FBIIC, the Assistant Secretary coordinates certain policies, procedures, and responses to crises for the Federal and State financial regulators. (See section 1.2 for further details.)

Additionally, to meet objectives set forth by HSPD–7 for collaboration with the private sector, the Treasury Department works closely with the private sector. Furthermore, the Secretary of the Treasury designates the private sector coordinator. (See section 1.2 for further details.)

1.1 Sector Profile

Financial institutions are organized and regulated based on the services the institutions provide. Therefore, the profile is best described by defining the services offered. These categories include: (1) deposit and payment systems and products; (2) credit and liquidity products; (3) investment products; and (4) risk transfer products. All aforementioned critical services are executed upon, or delivered through, IT-based platforms and channels; therefore cybersecurity components are factored into all critical infrastructure protection related activities performed by the sector.

The financial services sector is both large in assets and in the number of individual businesses. For example, in the sector there are: more than 18,800 federally insured depository institutions;[1] thousands of providers of various investment products, including roughly 18,440 broker-dealer, investment advisers, and investment company complexes;[2] providers of risk transfer products, including 7,948 domestic U.S. insurers;[3] and many thousands of other credit and financing organizations.

1.1.1 Deposit, Consumer Credit, and Payment Systems Products

Depository institutions of all types (i.e., banks, thrifts, and credit unions) are the primary providers of wholesale and retail payments services, such as wire transfers, checking accounts, and credit and debit cards. These institutions use and/or operate the payments infrastructure, which includes electronic large value transfer systems, automated clearinghouses (ACH), and automated teller machines (ATM). These institutions are the primary point of contact with the sector for many individual customers. Additionally, these institutions may be Federal or State-chartered banks or credit unions; however, in most instances, the Federal financial regulators have at least some authority over the institutions.

Along with the aforementioned payment systems, the depository institutions provide customers with various forms of extensions of credit, such as mortgages and home equity loans, collateralized and uncollateralized loans, and lines of credit, including credit cards. Consumers have multiple ways of accessing these services. For example, customers can make deposits in person at a depository institution's branch office, through the mail, at an ATM, or via direct deposit using ACH transactions. Customers can make withdrawals at a branch office, at an ATM, or by using a debit card or check. Customers also can access credit lines through other retail banking services using the telephone or the internet. In the United States, customers typically

---

[1] Available at **http://www2.fdic.gov/qbp/2009sep/qbp.pdf** and **www.ncua.gov/DataServices/Directory/2009/NCUA%20Directory-2009.pdf**.

[2] Available at **www.sec.gov/about/offices/ocie/ocie_offices.shtml**.

[3] Available at **http://www.naic.org/documents/research_stats_idrr_sample.pdf**.

have deposit, checking, and loan accounts with more than one depository institution. The average household may have up to 18 account relationships spread among 12 financial institutions.[4]

1.1.2 Credit and Liquidity Products

Customers seek liquidity and credit for a wide variety of needs. For example, individuals may seek a mortgage to purchase a home, businesses may obtain a line of credit to expand their operations, and governments may issue sovereign debt obligations. Many financial institutions, such as depository institutions, finance and lending firms, securities firms, and Government Sponsored Enterprises (GSEs) meet customers' long and short-term needs through a multitude of financial products. Some of these entities provide credit directly to the end customer, while others do so indirectly by providing wholesale liquidity to those financial services firms that provide these services on a retail basis.

Essential to the credit and liquidity market is the assurance that these products are available with integrity and fairness. The law provides for consumer protections against fraud involving these products, as well as certain other consumer protections, many of which are tied directly to the specific type of credit and liquidity product. Furthermore, credit and liquidity products are governed by a complex body of laws. These laws include Federal and State securities laws, banking laws, and laws that are tailored to the specifics of a particular class of lending activity.

1.1.3 Investment Products

Diversity of investment service providers and products promotes the global competitiveness of U.S. financial markets. These products provide opportunities for both short- or long-term investments and include debt securities (such as bonds and bond mutual funds) and equities (such as stocks or stock mutual funds), and derivatives (such as options and futures). Securities firms, depository institutions, pension funds, and GSEs all offer financial products that are used for investing needs. These investment products are issued and traded in various organized markets, from physical trading floors to electronic markets. Certain securities—U.S. Treasuries and equities of some multinational companies—are traded around the globe, 24 hours a day. The Treasury Department, the Securities and Exchange Commission (SEC), the Commodity Futures Trading Commission (CFTC), banking regulators, and insurance regulators all provide financial regulation for certain investment products. The SEC and CFTC have legally designated SROs. Notably, the SEC has the power to delegate authority to its SROs, national stock exchanges, and NASD to enforce certain industry standards and requirements related to securities trading and brokerage. Similarly, the CFTC oversees exchanges and the industry SRO, i.e., designated futures exchanges and the NFA, which have regulatory authority to enforce industry standards and requirements related to futures trading and participants. These regulatory requirements are directed toward consumer protection, fair and orderly markets, and the ongoing capability of financial services firms to meet their financial obligations.

1.1.4 Risk Transfer Products (Including Insurance)

The transfer of financial risks, such as the financial loss due to theft or the destruction of physical or electronic property resulting from a fire, cyber attack, or other loss event, or the loss of income due to a death or disability in a family, is an important tool for the sustainability of businesses and economic vitality of individuals and their families. A wide variety of financial institutions provide risk transference products to meet this market need.

The U.S. market for financial risk transfer products is among the largest in the world, measuring in the trillions of dollars. These products range from straightforward to exceedingly complex. For example, insurance companies, futures firms, and forward market participants offer financial products that allow customers to transfer various types of financial risks under a myriad of circumstances. Marketplace efficiency often requires that market participants engage in both financial investments as

---

[4] Sheshunoff Bank Profit Improvement Manual, October 2009.

well as in financial risk transfers that enable risk hedging. Financial derivatives, including futures and security derivatives, can provide both of these functions for market participants.

1.1.5 Federal and Self-Regulation of Financial Services Firms

All financial services firms are subject to the constraints of the financial market, and these markets have certain, though often informal, market constraints and self-regulation. Many of these financial firms are subject to additional governmental and legally mandated regulation and self-regulation. Such regulation is designed to provide reasonable assurance that consumers are protected, and that the financial services firm is able to meet its financial obligations on an ongoing basis. The U.S. financial regulatory system includes Federal and, in some cases, SROs concerned among other responsibilities with institutional and systemic ability to withstand operational disruptions.

1.1.6 State Regulation of Financial Services Firms

Some financial services may be regulated at both the Federal and State levels. Insurance services are unique in that they are primarily regulated by States. Under the McCarran-Ferguson Act of 1945,[5] Congress affirmed the right of the States exclusively to regulate the insurance industry. Except for a few Federal laws and regulations, State insurance commissioners generally have regulatory authority over all aspects of a firm's business, including rates and terms of policies, qualifications for licensing, market conduct, and financial structures and practices. (See appendix B for a listing of State statutory authorities.)

The chief insurance regulatory officials from each State collaborate through the National Association of Insurance Commissioners (NAIC). The NAIC is a member of the FBIIC. Many of the State insurance regulators review the disaster response and business continuity plans of insurers and conduct periodic examinations of these plans. The NAIC developed a handbook for State insurance regulatory response to disasters entitled, *The State Disaster Response Plan.*[6]

In addition to the insurance industry, State agencies regulate banks, thrifts, and credit unions that are State-chartered. Membership in the Federal Reserve System is optional for State-chartered banks, but all of the banks are insured by the Federal Deposit Insurance Corporation (FDIC). The Office of Thrift Supervision (OTS) also regulates State-chartered savings associations with FDIC-insured deposits. The National Credit Union Administration (NCUA) regulates State-chartered credit unions that have Federal deposit insurance. State agencies also regulate the purchase and sale of securities and the provision of investment advice regarding securities.

1.2 CIKR Partners

As the SSA for the Banking and Finance Sector, the Treasury Department recognizes the vital role of both the financial regulators and the private sector. These regulators and the private sector are committed to the Banking and Finance Sector's critical infrastructure and key resources (CIKR) partnership. Working collaboratively, this partnership achieves its security and resilience goals and addresses the evolving nature of both the sector and potential risks.

The Treasury Department has encouraged the collaboration of the sector's regulators, associations, and individual market participants through the FBIIC and a variety of private sector organizations. The Treasury Department and FBIIC members, working with private sector organizations: (1) share information at both the national and local levels; (2) assess and mitigate sector-wide risks; (3) develop and maintain key relationships; (4) conduct periodic testing of emergency protocols to be used during times of crisis; (5) establish research priorities; and (6) act as a focal point of information sharing between the public and private sectors.

---

[5]   15 USC § 1011 *et seq.*

[6]   Information is available at **http://www.naic.org/store_pub_naic_state.htm#state_drp**.

Furthermore, the Treasury Department works closely with the Department of Homeland Security (DHS) to seek high levels of resilience. As a member of various key working groups led by DHS, the Treasury Department has apprised DHS of situational priorities and remained fully engaged with DHS.

The Treasury Department and the FBIIC also share information with other Federal agencies on physical and cyber threats to the sector. In addition, the Treasury Department works with other statutory members of the intelligence community, the Department of Justice (DOJ), the U.S. Secret Service (U.S.S.S.), the Federal Bureau of Investigation (FBI), the National Communication System (NCS), as well as the 17 other CIKR sectors to gather and share information with the sector.[7]

1.2.1 Relationships with International, Federal, and State Regulators and Related Associations

The FBIIC is a standing subcommittee of the President's Working Group on Financial Markets (PWG) and is chaired by the Treasury Department's Assistant Secretary for Financial Institutions.[8] The FBIIC's role is to coordinate the efforts of Federal and State financial regulators with respect to financial services sector critical infrastructure issues, including preparation for, and response to, manmade or natural disasters of harm to the financial system or indirect attacks or events that may impact the sector.

The FBIIC has also reached out on a bilateral and multilateral basis to counterparts in other countries who are grappling with resilience issues. Federal regulators, for example, meet regularly through the auspices of international organizations and established inter-governmental groups to discuss issues of mutual concern that affect the stability of financial institutions and systems.

The FBIIC's membership includes regulators from the following agencies and associations:

FBIIC Members	
American Council of State Savings Supervisors (ACSSS)	National Association of State Credit Union Supervisors (NASCUS)
Board of Governors of the Federal Reserve System (FRB)	National Credit Union Administration (NCUA)
Commodity Futures Trading Commission (CFTC)	North American Securities Administrators Association (NASAA)
Conference of State Bank Supervisors (CSBS)	Office of the Comptroller of the Currency (OCC)
Farm Credit Administration (FCA)	Office of Thrift Supervision (OTS)
Federal Deposit Insurance Corporation (FDIC)	Securities and Exchange Commission (SEC)
Federal Housing Finance Agency (FHFA)	Securities Investor Protection Corporation (SIPC)
Federal Reserve Bank of New York (FRBNY)	U.S. Department of the Treasury
National Association of Insurance Commissioners (NAIC)	

---

[7] More information about all 18 CIKRs is available at http://www.dhs.gov/xprevprot/programs/gc_1189168948944.shtm.

[8] The PWG was established explicitly in response to events in the financial markets surrounding October 19, 1987, to give recommendations for legislative and private sector solutions for "enhancing the integrity, efficiency, orderliness, and competitiveness of [United States] financial markets and maintaining investor confidence". Executive Order No.12631 (1988). The PWG is chaired by the Secretary of the U.S. Department of the Treasury and includes the chairs of the Securities and Exchange Commission, the Commodity Futures Trading Commission, and the Board of Governors of the Federal Reserve System.

These agencies have regulatory authority over different sections of the financial services sector, and currently address infrastructure protection issues through routine regulatory interactions.

FBIIC members:

- Identify critical infrastructure assets and their locations, and prioritize their importance to the financial system;

- Establish secure communications capability and protocols for communicating among the financial regulators during an emergency;

- Identify the critical interdependencies of the Banking and Finance Sector with the Energy, Transportation, Communications, and IT Sectors; and

- Promote information sharing among and between the Federal, State, local, and tribal authorities, as well as the private sector.

The Treasury Department also has worked with Federal, State, local, and tribal law enforcement, including DHS and DOJ. Areas in which collaborative initiatives are being undertaken include:

- Providing protective response planning exercises designed to protect CIKR, and to create a response plan that incorporates State, local, and tribal law enforcement; and

- Enhancing communication and coordination across the sector.

As noted previously, FBIIC members possess extensive means to identify, assess, and assist with mitigating risks at the institutions within their legal purview. Their principal functions in the regulatory arena are described briefly below.

- The ACCSS is the national professional association of State-chartered savings institution regulators.

- The CFTC regulates futures commission merchants, including brokers, commodity trading advisors, commodity pool operators, futures markets, and derivatives clearing organizations. This is done in conjunction with exchanges such as the CME and the New York Mercantile Exchange, and the industry SRO, the NFA.

- The CSBS members regulate State-chartered banks.

- The FCA regulates the Farm Credit System.

- The FDIC regulates State-chartered banks that are not members of the Federal Reserve System and insured State branches of foreign banks.

- The FHFA is an independent agency established to regulate Fannie Mae, Freddie Mac, and Federal Home Loan Banks.

- The FRB regulates financial and bank holding companies and State-chartered member banks within the Federal Reserve System.

- The NAIC is an association of State insurance commissioners that regulate insurance companies and producers.

- NASCUS, a professional regulators association, is comprised of the 47 State agencies that charter, regulate, and examine the nation's State-chartered credit unions.

- The NCUA regulates federally chartered credit unions and shares some supervision responsibility with the State supervisory authorities for the federally insured, State-chartered credit unions.

- Members of the NASAA represent State securities regulators.

- The OCC regulates national banks and the Federal branches or agencies of foreign banks.

- The OTS regulates savings associations and savings and loan holding companies.

- The SEC regulates investment companies, investment advisors, broker-dealers, transfer agents, securities markets, and securities clearing organizations. This is done in conjunction with SROs such as the MSRB and FINRA.

- The Department of the Treasury is the President's leading policy advisor on a broad range of domestic and international economic issues.

1.2.2 Relationships with Private Sector Owners/Operators and Organizations

The Treasury Department has formed a strong bond with the private sector, including depository and lending institutions, as well as exchanges, trade associations, and other organizations within the sector.

The private sector is represented by several groups, including the Financial Services Sector Coordinating Council (FSSCC). The FSSCC and others meet periodically with the SSA and FBIIC and operates various committees addressing cybersecurity, research and development (R&D), and other issues of concern to the sector.

The Treasury Department, the FBIIC, and the financial services sector have encouraged and supported regional partnerships. In 2003, ChicagoFIRST became the first formal regional partnership within the financial sector, and it has since been followed by 17 other established partnerships and five developing partnerships in many areas of the country.

In 2007, a council of regional partnerships, called RPCfirst, was established. RPCfirst is a collective group of public-private partnerships that have formed across the United States to enhance the resilience of the financial sector in the face of disruptions, both manmade and natural.

1.3 Sector Goals and Objectives

The Banking and Finance Sector has an infrastructure that is designed to respond quickly and appropriately to detect, deter, prevent, and mitigate intrusions and attacks. This ability includes striving to ensure the continuity and efficient operation of the sector's institutions.

The Banking and Finance Sector's vision statement is as follows: "To continue to improve the resilience and availability of financial services, the Banking and Finance Sector will work through its public-private partnership to address the evolving nature of threats and the risks posed by the sector's dependency upon other critical sectors." To meet this vision, the Banking and Finance Sector has three primary goals:

1) To achieve the best possible position in the face of a myriad of intentional, unintentional, manmade, and natural threats against the sector's physical and cyber infrastructure;

2) To address and manage the risks posed by the dependence of the sector on the Communications, IT, Energy, and Transportation Systems Sectors; and

3) To work with the law enforcement community, financial regulatory authorities, the private sector, and our international counterparts to address threats facing the financial services sector.

2. Identify Assets, Systems, and Networks

Essential to conducting a risk assessment of the Banking and Finance Sector is the awareness that the products of the financial services industry are overwhelmingly not physical in nature. Thus, identifying and assessing assets in the sector is focused largely on identifying critical processes based on the organization of the sector as described in chapter 1, and the institutions that either own and operate or participate in these processes, rather than focusing on physical assets.

Vulnerability Assessment Methodology

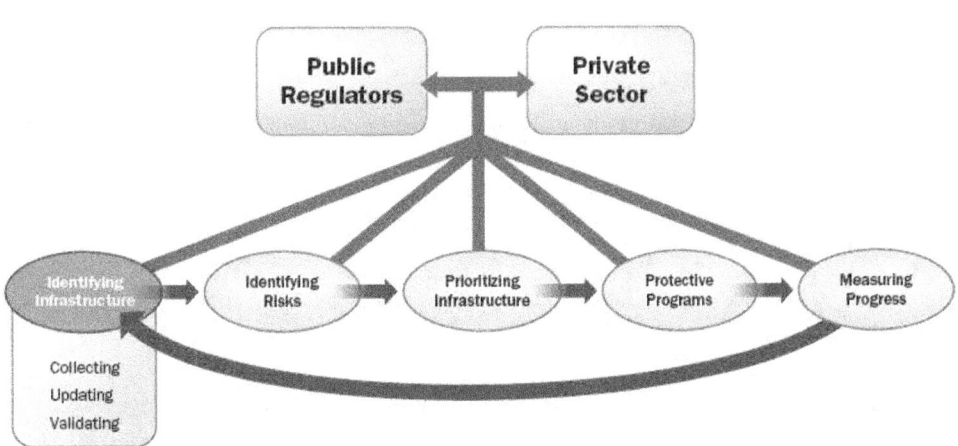

Many institutions play important roles in the financial system. Identifying institutions that have systemically critical operational roles is the first step to assuring their rapid recovery from a disruption of their critical functions, regardless of the cause. Identifying those institutions also is necessary for developing appropriate business continuity planning and recovery standards and ensuring compliance with those standards. After careful consideration, the Treasury Department and the FBIIC agencies identified a small number of systemically critical institutions whose operations form the backbone of the financial system.

There are also institutions or groups of institutions that, while not systemically critical, play significant roles in critical financial markets. Consequences of disruption at these organizations would vary. After September 11, 2001, the securities markets and several futures exchanges were closed until communications and other services were restored to lower Manhattan. The fact that these markets and new transactions were affected for a short period of time did not result in significant damage to or loss of confidence in the U.S. financial system.

Diversity within the financial services sector and geographic dispersion of its institutions foster significant resilience in the Banking and Finance Sector. In addition to the systemically critical institutions, the U.S. financial system consists of many thousands of depository institutions, securities and futures firms, insurance companies, and other financial service companies, and a number of exchanges and over-the-counter markets, all of which provide a high degree of redundancy across the sector. The competitive structure of the financial industry and the breadth of the financial instruments available also contribute to a level of resilience against attack and natural disaster. Thus, most of these institutions, while certainly important to the financial system, do not involve or pose systemic vulnerabilities and are not considered systemically critical.

2.1 Defining Information Parameters

The Banking and Finance Sector may be broken into several functions: deposit and payments systems; credit and liquidity products; investment products; and risk transfer products. Various members of the FBIIC regulate each of these functions, as outlined in chapter 1. Through their oversight authority, the financial regulators obtain vast amounts of information on institutions, critical assets and processes, and potential vulnerabilities. Sector-wide risk assessments are process driven and address interdependencies. Individual institutions conduct risk assessments for all critical business functions, including information security, to identify and mitigate internal vulnerabilities and external dependencies. The adequacy of risk assessment processes and methodologies is reviewed by the individual institution's primary regulator as part of the regulatory examination process.

The Treasury Department, through collaboration and insights obtained from the members of the FBIIC and the private sector, gathers sector-specific information.

General information for sector assets may include, as appropriate to each component of the sector, the following information:

- Asset name, mailing address, physical location, owner/operator name;
- Function or type of transaction—deposit and payments systems or credit and liquidity products, including investment and risk transfer;
- Geographic region, financial center;
- Number of people employed;
- Economic contribution—total market value of financial transactions conducted by or through the asset on a daily, weekly, monthly, and yearly basis;
- International considerations, if any;
- Existing and planned protective measures;
- Dependencies on other sectors such as Communications, Energy, IT, and Transportation Systems;
- Interaction with other assets—those other critical national assets directly and indirectly affected by the operation of each asset;
- Backup capability—the location and function of backup facilities (e.g., data center and business resumption); and
- Substitutability—whether other industry systems or infrastructures would be able to serve the same function.

Intangible assets, such as systems, databases, or networks, are in one way or another linked to physical assets and locations. Systemically significant assets are stratified by their regulatory agency with respect to criticality to the financial services sector as a whole.

2.2 Collecting Infrastructure Information

The Treasury Department and the Federal and State financial regulators' expertise in the financial services sector has been shaped by experience spanning most of the twentieth century, and far longer with respect to the Treasury Department. Continuous financial regulatory examinations and reporting requirements provide the financial regulatory agencies with voluminous and consistently updated data on institutions' operations and finances. Through the collaborative efforts of the FBIIC, the financial regulatory authorities have assessed the Banking and Finance Sector, identifying strengths and weaknesses within the domestic financial system, as well as pinpointing some institutions that play a systemically critical role within the sector.

2.2.1 Deposit and Payment System Products

The depository institution system is supported by electronic payment systems that link these institutions to one another and to their customers. Examples of these systems and networks are the many regional or national ATM networks[9] that permit consumers to access their funds from more than 1.7 million ATM sites worldwide;[10] four major credit card companies;[11] and the ACH operators, which processed more than 18.2 billion payments in 2008 (an increase of 1.2 billion over 2007)[12] Businesses and consumers increasingly use ACH payment systems to make recurring payments (e.g., creditor withdrawal of the customers' monthly mortgage and other recurring payments withdrawn by the appropriate creditor).

Several other payment systems, such as the Clearing House Interbank Payments System (CHIPS) and Fedwire, support larger value payments. In 2008, the Fedwire payments systems sent 131 million payments, valued at $755 trillion, over its system, with an average payment size of $5.75 million.[13] During the same period, CHIPS handled about 92 million transactions, valued at $508.8 trillion, with an average payment amounting to $5.5 million.[14] It is important to note that these systems may be linked to payments occurring in systems outside the United States.

In addition, the Depository Trust & Clearing Corporation, which is a clearing system for the equities and government securities markets across financial assets as diverse as equities, fixed income, OTC derivatives, mutual funds, and insurance products.[15] The Options Clearing Corporation, which provides futures and options clearing and settlement services for 10 exchanges, reported that total options volume across all exchanges finished at 3.6 billion contracts in 2008.[16]

Retail customers are increasingly processing their transactions with their depository institutions via the Internet. Financial regulators have issued extensive guidance to these institutions on how to manage this activity and mitigate the associated risks.

These deposit and payment system products are governed by a complex system of requirements, generally promulgated by Federal banking agencies, the SEC, or private SROs or rule-making bodies. The organizations operating payment systems are examined for compliance purposes by the appropriate agencies. For example, distinct Federal regulations govern the processing of funds stemming from checks, and inter-bank funds transfers, while ACH payments are governed by rules promulgated by NACHA-The Electronics Payment Association.

---

[9] ATM networks generally support both ATM and PIN-based debit card transactions.

[10] Available at **http://www.atmia.com/unitedstates/NewsDetail7.cfm?Id=0,106** Available at **http://www.atmia.com/unitedstates/NewsDetail7.cfm?Id=0,106**.

[11] These merchants have 55 million locations (merchants and ATMs) worldwide. The four major credit card companies are Visa, MasterCard, American Express, and Discover.

[12] Available at **http://www.nacha.org/News/news/pressreleases/2009/2009%20ACH%20Stats%20(Final).pdf**.

[13] Available at **http://www.federalreserve.gov/paymentsystems/fedfunds_ann.htm**.

[14] Available at **http://www.chips.org//docs/000652.pdf**.

[15] Available at **http://www.dtcc.com/downloads/annuals/2007/2007_report.pdf**.

[16] Available at **http://www.optionsclearing.com/components/doc/about/annual-reports/occ_2008_annual_report.pdf**.

2.2.2 Credit and Liquidity Products

Credit markets are not formal markets with either a physical location or one narrow set of methods that define them. Rather, there are a wide variety of financial firms that provide credit and financing, including the more than 18,800 depository institutions in the United States.[17] There are also a wide variety of non-depository providers, including mortgage financing firms and others. Moreover, many of the financial firms that provide financing at retail institutions require liquidity to fund their financing activity.

The number of financial services providers of credit and liquidity is extremely large due to the many specialized niche markets serviced, and the often highly tailored financial services provided. Given the many types of products offered, there is no single set of systems at work that dominates these financial products. However, throughout the entire financial services sector there are goals of safeguarding the assets of clients, and ensuring that client assets, the financial firms' assets, and recordkeeping systems are highly resilient to any foreseeable event.

2.2.3 Investment Products

Collectively, the thousands of investment service providers control trillions of dollars worth of financial assets. Many of these providers operate in a highly regulated environment governed by a complex legal structure.

Some of these investment products are provided on highly formalized financial markets, while others are provided by regulated financial services providers not acting specifically in a formal financial market. Examples of highly developed formal financial markets include financial exchanges, at which financial assets are traded in a tightly regulated manner so as to achieve the desired purposes of market participants.

These formal financial markets have highly developed and extremely technologically efficient redundant networks and systems that provide a high degree of resilience in the face of a variety of potential situations. Additionally, these networks provide both the customers and institutions with consistent access to their funds and records.

2.2.4 Risk Transfer Products

Risk transfer products include both insurance and hedging instruments such as futures and options. Life insurers reported having $5.1 trillion invested in the U.S. economy in 2007, in assets which back their life, annuity, and health liabilities.[18] Financial risk transfer products are often tailored to the unique nature of the risks involved, although there are numerous standardized financial risk transfer products, such as those traded on options and futures exchanges. The Options Clearing Corporation reported that $1.9 trillion in options premiums changed hands in 2008; and the year-end open interest notional value of contracts reached $2.0 trillion.[19] The networks and systems used by the institutions providing these services are often tailored to the individual financial firm.

2.2.5 Collecting Asset Data

To meet the challenge of more complex financial markets, products, and delivery systems, financial institutions—in particular, large financial institutions—have been implementing more formal and complex risk management systems. Similarly, the

---

[17] Available at **http://www2.fdic.gov/qbp/2009sep/qbp.pdf** and **www.ncua.gov/DataServices/Directory/2009/NCUA%20Directory-2009.pdf**.

[18] Available at **http://www.acli.com**; see "industry facts."

[19] 2007 Report Seasons of Growth, The Options Clearing Corporation. "Options premium" denotes the amount paid by the buyer of an option to the seller of an option. "Open interest" refers to contracts that are active on a specific underlying instrument, such as a security, but have not expired or been closed through a closing transaction or been terminated. Available at **http://www.optionsclearing.com/components/doc/about/annual-reports/occ_2008_annual_report.pdf** and **www.optionsclearing.com/components/docs/about/aaa_rating_09.pdf**.

regulators have refined their approach to supervision of financial institutions of all sizes by adopting a risk-focused approach to meet new challenges. Some regulators assign a staff of full-time examiners, who work on site, to the largest, most complex financial institutions. This on-site presence allows regulators to receive updated information about larger firms on a daily basis. Federal, and at times State, law gives financial regulatory agencies broad authority to access records held or maintained by regulated financial institutions.[20] That information generally is provided exclusively to the financial regulatory agency, although in the event of potential criminal law violations, mechanisms exist to share that information with law enforcement agencies, including those within DHS. The Treasury Department draws on many sources for asset data, as necessary.

2.3 Verifying Infrastructure Information

The Treasury Department, through the members of the FBIIC, uses a three-part process to verify physical and cyber asset information. First, a drafting committee collects and verifies the information. Second, the FBIIC members review the information for accuracy and errors. Third, a special FBIIC review committee subjects each asset assessment to rigorous questioning and review.

2.4 Updating Infrastructure Information

The information gathered through the examination process provides access to infrastructure information on the Banking and Finance Sector. Sector institutions are typically examined over a period of 12 to 18 months, thus providing updated information to the Banking and Finance Sector. In addition, the Treasury Department, through the members of the FBIIC, updates asset data on an as-needed basis. Data collected through the regulatory processes of individual agencies are maintained and secured by each agency and shared, to the extent possible, as allowed by statutory and regulatory requirements.

---

[20] Some of those sources of Federal statutory authority are contained in Titles 12 and 15 of the United States Code. (See appendix B for further details.)

3. Assess Risks

Both the public and private members of the Banking and Finance Sector conduct risk assessments. These assessments look at issues and potential vulnerabilities both within individual organizations and sector-wide. Since risk management is part of the banking and finance culture, both regulators and private organizations have a long history of conducting regular risk assessments. In the private sector, some of these risk assessments are mandated through regulation and validated by the examination process.

Following the attacks of September 11, 2001, the FBIIC was created and began an organized effort to examine the financial sector's resilience. The process has continued and matured over the years to include physical and cyber-based components of the sector as well as dependencies on other critical sectors. Information in this process is garnered through the regulators' knowledge of sector participants. Information shared between the members of the sector and the financial regulators provides insights into the operational and systemic risks facing individual organizations and the sector as a whole. Through organizations such as the Federal Financial Institutions Examination Council (FFIEC) and the FBIIC, there is ongoing verification and validation updating of risk assessment information.

Through this process, the Treasury Department has identified potential limitations, and created a process to identify and assess vulnerabilities within the sector. The following sections refer to the efforts of the Treasury Department, working with the FBIIC members and the private sector, to identify sector vulnerabilities and assess the risks across the Banking and Finance Sector.

Vulnerability Assessment Methodology

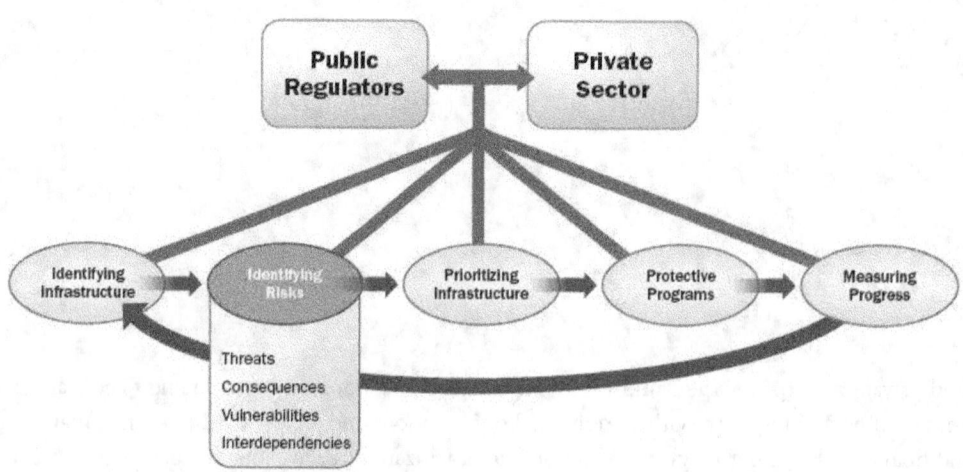

3.1 Use of Risk Assessment in the Sector

The Banking and Finance Sector has a long-standing and accepted practice of conducting risk assessments and mitigating vulnerabilities. While many risk assessments are conducted by the private sector to satisfy regulatory requirements, private sector entities have access to methodologies and best practices provided by trade groups and, for certain parts of the sector, SROs. These risk assessments appropriately take into account the National Infrastructure Protection Plan (NIPP) core criteria, including consequences, vulnerabilities, and threats to the essential underlying clearing, payment, and settlements systems of the sector. These assessments also consider vulnerabilities stemming from direct or indirect threats to the operations across the sector. Furthermore, these assessments consider the nature of the incident, whether natural or manmade. The focus of these sector-wide assessments is on the potential impact that such risks, if exploited, would have on the orderly and efficient operation of the sector.

Each regulatory agency examines the individual entities within its purview based upon a risk management framework. Consequence analysis in risk assessment methodologies in the public sector include the potential economic impact, the impact on public confidence in the financial system, and the impact on the government's ability to continue to provide its services to the public.

Collectively, the public sector, under the auspices of the FBIIC, carefully analyzes the entire U.S. financial system to assess its strength and resilience to manmade and natural disasters. Relying upon their collective expertise and experience, the members of the FBIIC developed a risk assessment methodology for the Banking and Finance Sector. Based on this methodology, the FBIIC agencies identify financial institutions that play significant roles in key financial markets either individually or as a group. The vulnerability assessments address physical and cyber weaknesses in the financial services sector and are representative of both kinds of incidents. These risk assessments come together to provide an overall risk profile of the sector.

In addition to Banking and Finance Sector led assessments, DHS has conducted risk assessments for the sector. In 2009, DHS' Protective Security Advisors (PSAs), in conjunction with ChicagoFIRST, conducted an assessment of physical infrastructure within the City of Chicago's financial district.

3.2 Screening Infrastructure

As stated in chapter 1, the Banking and Finance Sector may be broken into several functions: deposit and payments systems; credit and liquidity products; investment products; and risk transfer products. The Treasury Department and members of the FBIIC use a screening process to identify certain assets within the Banking and Finance Sector that are systemically important.

The sector is constantly changing, as are the dynamic screening efforts of the FBIIC to identify these systemically important assets. The Treasury Department and the FBIIC continually meet with financial institutions and regulators to assess whether any new assets are critical to the operations of the sector. When a new asset is identified, the Treasury Department and the FBIIC take appropriate actions to address any vulnerability related to that asset.

The described asset data are controlled by the Treasury Department and the members of the FBIIC. The Treasury Department and key stakeholders in the public and private sectors update the asset data on an as-needed basis.

3.3 Assessing Consequences

The Banking and Finance Sector assesses the consequences of an asset's loss or impairment within the context of its impact on the sector's ability to operate efficiently and in an orderly manner and its potential impact on the public's confidence in the financial system as a whole. Several factors used in this assessment include: diversity; redundancy; nature of dependence on the asset, network, or system; and symbolic importance.

3.4 Assessing Vulnerabilities

The Banking and Finance Sector conducts ongoing vulnerability assessments. These vulnerability assessments include examinations into the potential risks resulting from cross-sector dependence, sector-specific vulnerabilities, and dependencies on key assets, systems, technologies, and processes. These assessments are based upon the extensive knowledge of regulators and guidance issued, and takes into account physical, cyber, and human vulnerabilities, available redundancy, and the sector's reliance on sector-specific assets, systems, and processes—and cross-sector reliance on these factors. Consequence assessments are based on expert judgment.

Through the vulnerability assessments, the sector has determined that some of its greatest challenges arise from its dependence on the telecommunications network and IT.

Dependency Relationships

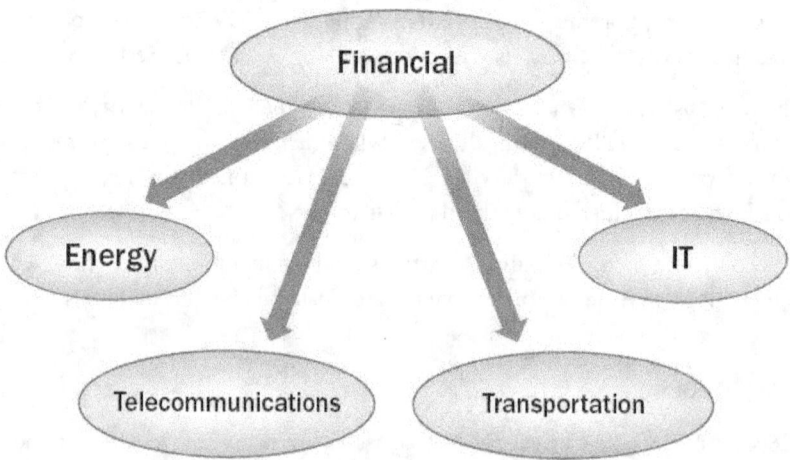

Any vulnerability assessment of the financial services sector cannot be truly final because the sector is evolving constantly. Thus, the FBIIC members continue to update assessments regularly to identify vulnerabilities and manage and assess asset risks, especially as the sector adopts new technology. Furthermore, the Treasury Department has been working with DHS to coordinate how to normalize the results of the Banking and Finance Sector's vulnerability assessments so that they may be comparable to the overall NIPP.

3.5 Assessing Threats

There have been individuals and groups that have attempted to exploit the sector for their own pecuniary gains. Over time, the sector has developed defenses to thwart these attacks. However, criminals continue to devise new methods and schemes. Therefore, the Treasury Department works with other Federal agencies, including the intelligence community and DHS, to assess physical and cyber threats that are identified as specifically directed at the sector or at an asset on a national, regional, or local level. Relationships with DHS, the intelligence community, and other SSAs provide real-time information regarding these threats. Additionally, when threats are identified, frequent communications between the FBIIC and the private sector facilitate efficient and effective transfer of potential threat information, permitting the sector to mitigate the associated vulnerabilities.

The DHS Homeland Infrastructure Threat and Risk Analysis Center (HITRAC) conducts integrated threat analysis for CIKR sectors, and is working with the Banking and Finance Sector. HITRAC brings together intelligence and infrastructure specialists to ensure complete and sophisticated understanding of risks to U.S. CIKR.

Because cyber threats are a significant concern of the sector, the Treasury Department works with the U. S. Computer Emergency Readiness Team (US-CERT) to identify the latest threats to cyber infrastructure and disseminates threat information within the sector.

4. Prioritize Infrastructure

The Treasury Department, in conjunction with the members of the FBIIC undertakes periodic efforts to identify and prioritize the key infrastructure. The prioritization within this approach assists the sector in determining the focus for protective programs.

The Treasury Department, through outreach to the members of the FBIIC, has conducted risk assessment reviews of the sector. This effort has provided a sector-wide prioritization focused on business continuity and resilience for essential processes in the Banking and Finance Sector in the event of an attack or natural disaster. The prioritization is informed by the extensive knowledge of the members of the FBIIC and, where appropriate, in consultation with certain private sector owners and operators. As the sector is changing constantly, so too are the Treasury Department's and the FBIIC's processes for identifying and prioritizing the systemically important assets, processes, and networks. The Treasury Department and the FBIIC meet with financial institutions and regulators to assess whether any new assets are critical to the operations of the sector. Results from these consultations are used to update the prioritization where and when appropriate.

The Treasury Department uses the prioritization to inform sector participants, where appropriate, and to facilitate discussions, if necessary, to employ protective measures with the owners and operators. In specific instances, the Treasury Department has reached out to these members of the sector to encourage participation in business continuity exercises and programs by the FBIIC.

Furthermore, the Treasury Department works with its sector partners, including DHS and the intelligence community, to collaborate on threat analysis and information dissemination in accordance with the prioritization in the Banking and Finance Sector. This process enables the coordination necessary to conform with NIPP core criteria and helps to facilitate DHS's efforts to assess national comparable risk.

The basis for prioritization of critical infrastructure within the Banking and Finance Sector stems from the degree of sector reliance on the identified assets, processes, and networks. Analysis for this prioritization relies upon the potential impact on the sector's continued efficient and orderly operation should the critical infrastructure experience significant interruption or loss. Essential to this prioritization process is the importance that these infrastructure and the overall financial services system have in maintaining the public's confidence in our national economic system and political institutions. The prioritization effort incorporates a variety of factors, including the:

- Degree of industry dependence on the asset;
- Presence or absence of alternative suppliers of the services performed by the asset;
- Public need for the services provided by the asset;
- Potential impact of a disruption on the asset to the financial system;

- Potential impacts on the economy through the cascading disruption of other CIKR; and

- Trends and specific information in threat analysis.

As an example of prioritization, after the September 11th attacks, the Federal Reserve System, Office of the Comptroller of the Currency and Securities Exchange Commission issued an interagency white paper addressing sound practices to strengthen the resilience of the U.S. financial system. The goal of this document was to ensure that key organizations in critical financial markets were able to recover clearing and settlement activities in the event of a wide scale disruption.[21]

Vulnerability Assessment Methodology

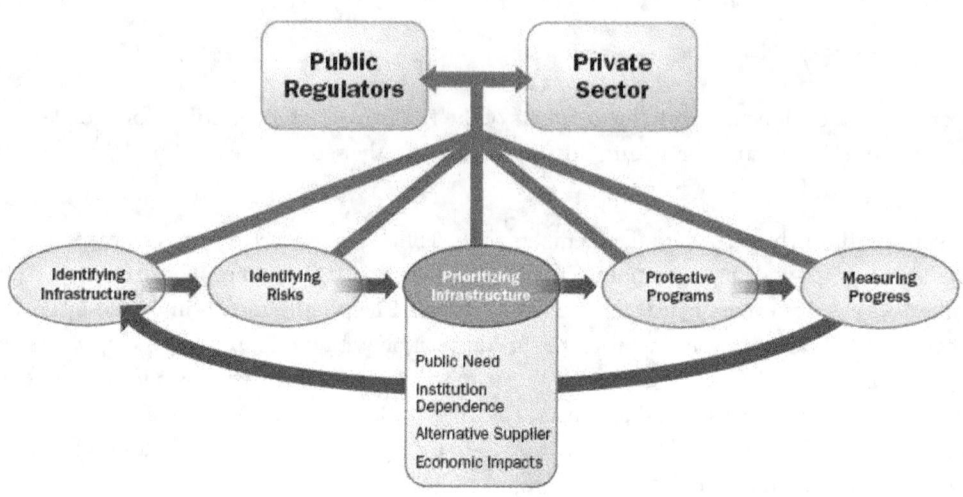

[21] The Interagency White Paper on Sound Practices to Strengthen the Resilience of the U.S. Financial System. Available at http://www.sec.gov/news/studies/34-47638.htm.

5. Develop and Implement Protective Programs and Resilience Strategies

5.1 Overview of Sector Protective Programs and Resilience Strategies

Due to the highly diverse and decentralized nature of the Banking and Finance Sector, and the fact that the sector is largely owned and operated by the private sector, public and private sector owners and operators must share the responsibility for ensuring the orderly and efficient operation of the sector and meeting the sector's security and resilience goals.

5.2 Determining the Need for Protective Programs and Resilience Strategies

Through both direct mandates and regulatory authority the public sector plays an essential role in the development of private sector protective programs. For the public sector, the FBIIC, an organization of 17 financial sector regulatory agencies, is charged with encouraging coordination and communication among financial regulators, enhancing the resilience of the financial sector, and promoting the public-private partnership.

The private sector is involved in identifying the need for protective programs and resilience strategies through various groups, including the FSSCC. The FSSCC both collaborates with the FBIIC on resilience efforts and also engages in independent efforts based on its members' identification of industry security needs.

The Treasury Department has an established program to identify cross-sector interdependencies. For example, the SSA has worked with NCS and other telecommunication partners to identify gaps in protection. In addition, the SSA has collaborated with the participants from the Communications, IT, Defense Industrial Base, Energy, and Transportation Systems Sectors to determine the necessary level of redundancy and assurance.

5.3 Protective Program/Resilience Strategy Implementation

The Treasury Department, the FBIIC, and the private sector have protective program initiatives and resilience strategies that seek to address the sector goals listed in chapter 1. These goal oriented programs, projects and initiatives are described in some detail below.

> **Goal 1:** To achieve the best possible position in the face of a myriad of intentional, unintentional, manmade, and natural threats against the sector's physical and cyber infrastructure.

The FBIIC is a formal information-sharing organization for the financial regulatory community, which includes both cross subsector representation and Federal authorities and associations of State regulatory authorities. The FBIIC:

- Meets to discuss progress on research, exercises, protective measures, and emerging risks, and to identify new means for continuing the progress towards improving the resilience of the sector; and

- Coordinates with foreign regulatory agencies to improve emergency preparedness of critical financial institutions.

The Treasury Department and the FBIIC, jointly have:

- Developed emergency management communication protocols for information sharing during a crisis, with quarterly testing of protocols;

- Shared information from various alert services and disseminated such information through established communication protocols;

- Built relationships with law enforcement and the intelligence community to monitor new and emerging threats and to mitigate those threats and vulnerabilities;

- Brought together U.S. and international financial organizations and regulators to discuss the impact of pandemic business continuity planning on the global financial market; and

- In addition, through its strong private-public partnerships, the Treasury Department collaborates with the FBIIC and the private sector on sector-wide exercises.

Goal 2: To address and manage the risks posed by the dependence of the sector on the Communications, IT, Energy, and Transportation Systems Sectors.

The financial regulators and the private sector are:

- Examining, with other Federal partners, the financial sector's reliance on telecommunications infrastructure;

- Working with other critical infrastructure sectors and appropriate government agencies to address critical interdependencies including telecommunications diversity and resilience, and electrical power grid vulnerabilities;

- Sponsoring private sector firms that qualify under the national security and emergency preparedness guidelines for participation in Government Emergency Telecommunications Systems (GETS), Wireless Priority Service (WPS), and Telecommunications Service Priority (TSP) programs. The GETS and WPS grant users priority access over the telecommunications public network during emergencies;

- Drafted emergency communications procedures allowing communications between financial regulators and Federal, State, and local CIKR partners;

- Sponsoring key private sector partners for clearances allowing access to classified threat information;

- Working on the issue of dependence on other sectors such as Transportation, Communications, IT, and Energy;

- Issuing guidance and conducting regular examinations of institutions' risk management of IT, including system design, software design and management, hardware design and management, use of services and their service level agreements, and use of assurance products and services;

- Working with Communications Sector participants to assess the vulnerability of the Communications Sector on which the financial sector is primarily dependent;

- Communicating on a regular basis with the IT, Energy, Transportation Systems, and Communication Sectors on issues that impact the Banking and Finance Sector;

- Meeting with and continuing to build relationships with representatives from the other sectors through the Partnership for Critical Infrastructure Security (PCIS); and

- In addition, the financial regulators are serving as members of the Government Coordinating Councils (GCCs) for the IT, Communications, Defense Industrial Base, and Energy Sectors.

Goal 3: To work with the law enforcement community, financial regulatory authorities, the private sector, and our international counterparts to address threats facing the financial services sector.

The Treasury Department and members of the FBIIC have:

- Participated in DHS cyber-based exercises such as "Cyber Storm I" and in 2008 "Cyber Storm II" with the National Cyber Response Coordination Group (NCRCG), and have been involved in the initial planning meetings for Cyber Storm III;

- Worked with DHS and RPCfirst to develop and pilot a cyber exercise for use by the regional coalitions;

- Worked with DHS to provide Buffer Zone Protection Plans for critical institutions;

- Met with and support the efforts of Federal law enforcement including the DOJ and the U.S.S.S.;

- Worked collaboratively with other CIKR sectors to accomplish DHS's Cross-Sector Cyber Security Working Group activities; and

- Arranged for security briefings by U.S. intelligence and law enforcement officials for FBIIC and FSSCC members, as appropriate.

Going Forward

The financial services sector is dependent upon the collaboration and participation of the sector participants. The public-private partnership helps to strengthen the resilience of the sector only if there is trust and cooperation between the public and private participants. Therefore, the Treasury Department coordinates with members of the FBIIC and the private sector to validate, update, and implement metrics for the financial services sector, as necessary.

The Treasury Department, in the role of the SSA, and its public and private sector partners have conducted and facilitated various actions to achieve the Banking and Finance Sector's security and resilience goals. The following lists exemplify these efforts as they relate to the sector metrics and goals.

Goal 1: To achieve the best possible position in the face of a myriad of intentional, unintentional, manmade, and natural threats against the sector's physical and cyber infrastructure.

The Treasury Department, as the SSA, works with the appropriate members of the FBIIC and the private sector to:

- Sponsor private sector firms that qualify under the national security and emergency preparedness guidelines for GETS, WPS, and TSP;

- Participate in national and regional exercises to test and enhance the resilience of the financial services sector, such as the Banking and Finance Sector participation in Top Officials (TOPOFF) 4 and assistance in the planning process for the National Level Exercise program;

- Conduct briefings for the public and private stakeholders on the latest intelligence and threat assessments;

- Work with the sector participants to conduct tests to strengthen the response protocols for the FBIIC;

- Work with international organizations to look at issues related to financial management of large-scale disasters;

- Conduct the appropriate review and update process by the Treasury Department and the FBIIC agencies for asset data on the sector; and

- Encourage the financial services sector participants to develop, enhance, and test business continuity plans. Financial regulators have created and mandate stringent business recovery guidelines for their regulated institutions, such as the March 2008, FFIEC IT Handbook on Business Continuity Planning.[22] In some cases the regulators, in their "Interagency White Paper," have specified recovery timeframes for core clearing and settlement institutions (two hours) and significant players (four hours) in the event of a regional disaster.[23]

> **Goal 2:** To address and manage the risks posed by the dependence of the sector on the Communications, IT, Energy, and Transportation Systems Sectors.

The Treasury Department, as the SSA, has collaborated with the appropriate FBIIC members. Collaborative efforts have involved:

- Inviting participants from other sectors, including the Communications, IT, Energy, and Transportation Systems Sectors, to the general and working group meetings of the FBIIC to foster information sharing regarding cross-sector vulnerabilities and protective measures;

- Participating on the GCCs of other sectors, where permitted and appropriate;

- Working with NCS and other telecommunication partners to identify gaps;

- Working with the participants from the Communications, IT, Energy, and Transportation Systems Sectors to determine the necessary level of redundancy and assurance to meet the vision statement of the Banking and Finance Sector; and

- Utilizing the regional financial partnerships to coordinate discussions with State and local emergency managers and other sector partners.

> **Goal 3:** To work with the law enforcement community, financial regulatory authorities, the private sector, and our international counterparts to address threats facing the financial services sector.

---

[22] Available at **http://www.ffiec.gov/ffiecinfobase/booklets/bcp/bus_continuity_plan.pdf**.
[23] Ibid.

The Treasury Department, as the SSA, joined the appropriate members of the FBIIC to:

- Communicate with US-CERT, the U.S. intelligence community, and law enforcement community to share information on cybersecurity threats that may directly or indirectly impact the sector;

- Plan briefings between law enforcement and the financial services regulators and the private sector on the occasion of specific instances of cyber crimes;

- Coordinate with DHS to sponsor security clearances for need-to-know personnel within the financial services sector to facilitate the sharing of relevant information affecting the sector; and

- Support a private sector R&D initiative which is researching how to make financial services systems more resilient against cyber threats.

5.4 Monitoring Program Implementation

The Banking and Finance Sector's protective programs and resilience strategies are continuously monitored and assessed, and remedial actions taken as necessary to ensure that relevant risks are adequately addressed. Sector partners responsible for implementation of specific protective programs and resilience strategies are also principally responsible for monitoring the effectiveness of these programs. Robust Federal and State regulatory examination programs, in addition to continuous coordination and information sharing among all partners through the FBIIC, FSSCC, and other forums, enable the identification of protective programs and resilience strategies.

The Treasury Department and members of the FBIIC, along with private sector participants, developed several protective programs, including programs specific to cybersecurity and pandemic planning. Examples of protective program performance successes are detailed below.

- During 2006, the Treasury Department and members of the FBIIC completed an updated vulnerability assessment of the sector;

- The Treasury Department leads regular testing of the emergency communication system of the FBIIC;

- The FBIIC works on issues concerning dependence on other sectors such as Transportation Systems, Communications, IT, and Energy;

- The Treasury Department sponsors, organizes, and encourages participation at outreach meetings for financial services representatives across the country regarding infrastructure protection issues, including how the FBIIC and the private sector operate as national partnerships and how regional coalitions are an important part of the national strategy; and

- The Treasury Department chairs efforts of the FBIIC and communicates with the FSSCC Cyber Security Working Group and the group's various subcommittees. The Cyber Security Working Group is currently evolving and will align its structure to meet future priorities and needs of the sector.

6. Measure Effectiveness

6.1 Risk Mitigation Activities

In the preceding chapters, this 2010 SSP catalogues the activities undertaken by the Banking and Finance Sector to identify assets, assess risks, and develop and implement appropriate protective actions and resilience strategies.

The Treasury Department, in its role as the SSA, has been working with the FBIIC to collect the necessary information for descriptive, process, and outcome metrics. Because of the great diversity within the financial services sector, the Treasury Department must rely on the expertise and knowledge of the financial regulatory agencies for information on the assets within their purview.

Vulnerability Assessment Methodology

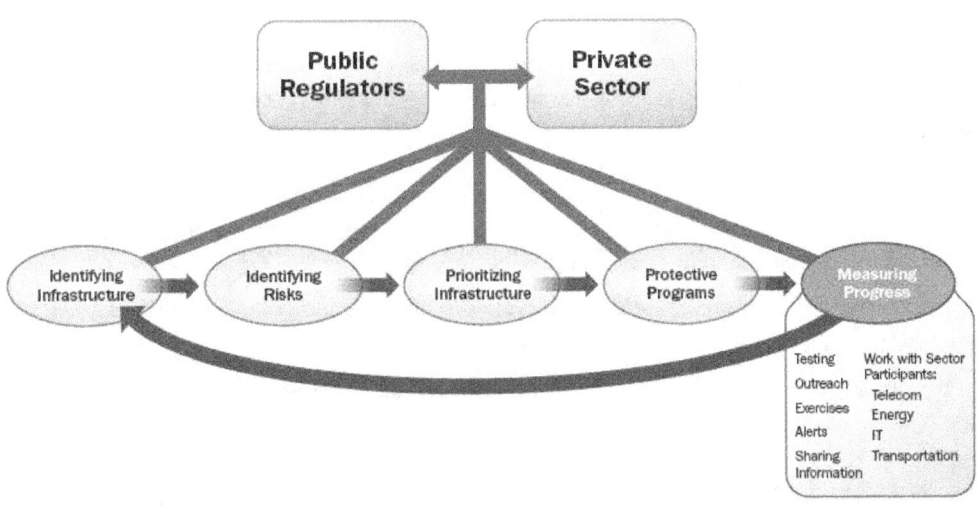

6.2 Process for Measuring Effectiveness

As the SSA for the Banking and Finance Sector, the Treasury Department is working with the FBIIC and the private sector to create suitable sector metrics as a means to measure the effectiveness of protective programs and resilience strategies. Measurements of the resilience efforts in a large and diverse sector, such as the Banking and Finance Sector, are difficult to quantify using standard business measurements. Therefore, a one-size-fits-all approach would be inapplicable to all aspects of the sector and also would weaken creativity and vitality in the sector, which would harm the nation's overall economy.

As evidenced by previous sections of this document, the Treasury Department has already done significant work in developing and collecting descriptive and process metrics. The Treasury Department continued to develop and collect meaningful outcome and baseline metrics and measurements that are relevant for the subsectors within the Banking and Finance Sector.

> **Goal 1:** To achieve the best possible position in the face of a myriad of intentional, unintentional, manmade, and natural threats against the sector's physical and cyber infrastructure.

The Treasury Department, as the SSA, supports members of the FBIIC in efforts to determine:

- The appropriate review and update processes by the Treasury Department and the FBIIC agencies for asset data on the sector; and

- The level of support needed to improve business continuity plans for national disasters.

> **Goal 2:** To address and manage the risks posed by the dependence of the sector on the Communications, IT, Energy, and Transportation Systems Sectors.

The Treasury Department, as the SSA, has been working with the appropriate members of the FBIIC to determine:

- The level of collaboration with GCCs and Sector Coordinating Councils (SCCs) of the Communications, IT, Energy, and Transportation Systems Sectors as well as specific industry participants to identify concerns and foster information sharing regarding cross-sector vulnerabilities and protective measures;

- The level of collaboration with the NCS and other telecommunications partners to identify gaps;

- The necessary level of redundancy and assurance from the Communications, IT, Energy, and Transportation Systems Sectors to meet the vision statement of the Banking and Finance Sector;

- The level of participation in and support for pandemic exercises to pinpoint areas of concern where the financial services sector depends upon the infrastructure of other sectors; and

- The level of coordination between regional coalitions and State and local emergency managers and other sector partners.

> **Goal 3:** To work with the law enforcement community, financial regulatory authorities, the private sector, and our international counterparts to address threats facing the financial services sector.

The Treasury Department, as the SSA, has worked with the appropriate members of the FBIIC to determine:

- The appropriate level of security clearances for members of the private sector to participate in briefings on threats to the sector;

- The current level of resilience within the sector in order to develop recommendations for best practices, education, policy, and exercises to strengthen the sector's resilience to cyber threats; and

- The ways to identify and increase awareness of emerging technologies that may assist with combating cyber crime or that may be used by criminal elements.

6.2.1 Information Collection and Verification

As previously stated, the Federal and State financial regulators gather a wide range of information on their regulated institutions for a variety of purposes; therefore, the Treasury Department coordinates with the members of the FBIIC to gather appropriate core metrics information on the Banking and Finance Sector. For example, the Treasury Department confers with the OCC for appropriate information on national banks; the NCUA for appropriate information on Federally-insured credit unions; the SEC for appropriate information on investment advisors, brokers/dealers, and securities markets; and the CFTC for appropriate information on futures commission merchants, commodity pool operators, and futures markets. The financial regulators regularly obtain data from their regulated entities and have appropriate protection measures in place to safeguard such information. The Treasury Department also validates the information with the appropriate private sector participants.

Once these core metrics are identified, the Treasury Department and the FBIIC have been examining the issue of the possibility of a method to create a system that can be used to assess how these metrics will be measured for the sector. This assessment has been based on regulators' extensive knowledge of the organizations within the sector, the technology employed by the sector, and the laws and regulations that apply to the sector. Furthermore, the Treasury Department and the FBIIC agencies have worked directly with each specific metric to consider how to validate, assess, and update the metric as necessary. On an annual basis, the Treasury Department and the FBIIC agencies have reviewed the assessment methodology and each metric outcome to determine whether the metric may be the appropriate metric for the future.

6.2.2 Reporting

As the SSA for the Banking and Finance Sector, the Treasury Department continues to work within the reporting structure identified by HSPD-7 to provide information and expertise to DHS.

6.3 Process for Measuring Effectiveness

As part of the overall NIPP, the Banking and Finance SSP provides the strategy for public and private sector partners to work together to identify, prioritize, and coordinate the protection of critical infrastructure. This update to the 2007 Banking and Finance SSP also summarizes the extensive activities that the sector has done and continues to do to reduce vulnerabilities and share information. As the SSA, the Treasury Department has the responsibility to promote the implementation of the Banking and Finance SSP. Given the dynamic nature of the sector, the Treasury Department has worked closely with the FBIIC, the private sector, and its CIKR partners to create dynamic implementation actions that allow the update to the SSP to be flexible and adaptive.

6.4 Using Metrics for Continuous Improvement

The evolving nature of the Banking and Finance Sector poses a unique challenge to the Treasury Department and its public and private sector partners to continually update these metrics. The Treasury Department and its public and private sector partners must maintain awareness of emerging technologies and vulnerabilities that the sector may face to determine whether the metrics remain appropriate for the sector. Another challenge for the sector is addressing and managing the risks associated with the sector's interdependencies. As the SSA, the Treasury Department has continued to work with the GCCs of other sectors to mitigate these risks and collaborate on creative solutions.

7. CIKR Protection Research and Development

7.1 Overview of Sector R&D

At the request of the Treasury Department, the private sector FSSCC has formed an R&D committee to develop plans and programs that would provide the most significant benefits with respect to the specific CIKR requirements of the financial services sector. In 2006, this committee issued a list of research challenges that provide information security professionals with insights with which they may be able to address known vulnerabilities in the sector. The FSSCC R&D committee revised the priorities paper in early 2008 by consolidating nine research and development challenges into seven, re-evaluating the priority order, and seeking input from experts in academic, governmental, financial services, and IT communities.[24] This work is continuing into 2010.

7.2 Sector R&D Requirements

Vast networks of information technology systems support the Banking and Finance Sector. These systems are composed of networks, servers, mainframes, operating systems, and software applications. The sector uses some of the most advanced technologies available to process billions of transactions each day, such as trade orders, clearing and settlements transactions, custody, account balances, and retail payments. Information systems may be rendered unavailable by either cyber or physical attacks. Compromises to the financial services sector's IT systems may affect sector operations and thus public trust and confidence in the U.S. economy.

In addition to IT systems, the Banking and Finance Sector is also heavily dependent on telecommunications. Given a wide-scale disruption of the telecommunications infrastructure, the Banking and Finance Sector would likely be unable to maintain critical voice and data communications at the level necessary to assure continuity of critical operations. Likewise, the financial service sector participants are interdependent. Therefore, a localized disruption that impacts a systemically critical organization may also result in cascading disruptions of trading, settlement, and payment activities across the country and in foreign markets.

The FSSCC R&D committee identified seven areas which may present significant issues for the financial sector in meeting its challenges in the coming years. The areas are:

- Advancing the state of the art in designing and testing secure applications;
- The security and resilience of financial transaction systems;
- Improvement in enrollment and identity credential management;

---

[24] See appendix C for the 2008 FSSCC R&D Agenda, which is available at **https://www.fsscc.org/fsscc/reports/2008/RD_Agenda-FINAL.pdf**.

- Understanding the human insider threat;
- Data-centric protection strategies;
- Measures of the value of security investments; and
- Development of practical standards.

The impact and timing of trends contributing to the challenges have been assessed and recommendations made for research that would support the financial services industry. In response to several of the major gaps and challenges of financial sector R&D, in 2007 the FSSCC established a program to connect experts within the Banking and Finance Sector with researchers in academia: the Subject Matter Advisory Response Team (SMART) program. The program assists R&D organizations working on critical infrastructure protection projects by providing subject matter expertise from financial institutions necessary to facilitate this R&D.[25]

7.3 Sector R&D Plan

In 2006, the FSSCC R&D committee began an effort to build upon the sector's research challenges. In 2008, the committee updated its financial services sector research agenda demonstrating how FSSCC research challenges relate to the NIPP. Details of the 2008 research agenda are provided in appendix C.

It is apparent from the analysis of both documents that there are many areas common to the NIPP and FSSCC R&D research programs and that with minor modifications the two programs could be synchronized to mutual benefit. Especially noteworthy are the following potential national areas for R&D that could have the most impact on the financial services sector:

- Protection and prevention systems;
- Advanced infrastructure architecture; and
- Human and social issues.

The FSSCC R&D committee recommends that research in these areas be given national priority and stands ready to assist in developing a coordinated plan with the overall NIPP program.

7.4 R&D Management Processes

The Department of the Treasury has been working with the critical information infrastructure protection interagency working group on the draft of the physical and cyber portion of the National CIP R&D Strategy. The Treasury Department has exchanged facts and information with numerous individuals and organizations both inside and outside of the sector to identify R&D projects that will benefit the financial services sector with the goal of making the sector more resilient against both external and internal threats. The Treasury Department believes that this pragmatic approach is the best method of making the sector more secure.

The FSSCC R&D committee is organized to support R&D initiatives to ensure the protection and resilience of the physical and electronic infrastructure of the Banking and Finance Sector's activities that are vital to the nation's economic well-being. The committee provides guidance for the creation of an FSSCC R&D agenda to identify and prioritize areas of need. The committee also provides industry, research/academia, and the public insights into the opportunities and related requirements. Further, the committee facilitates the coordination of financial services sector-wide R&D voluntary activities and initiatives designed to improve the sector's critical infrastructure protection and resilience.

---

[25] SMART program is available at **https://www.fsscc.org/fsscc/reports/2008/SMART_Program.pdf**.

The FSSCC R&D committee operates with a charter to support the following:

- Creation of an FSSCC R&D agenda to identify and prioritize the areas of need, in which the most promising opportunities can be found for research, and development initiatives to significantly improve the financial services sector's critical infrastructure protection;

- Publication of updates as needed to documentation of the FSSCC R&D agenda, to provide industry, research/academia, and the public with a shared insight into the opportunities and requirements;

- Provision of guidance for the process by which research proposals are selected and funded;

- Provision of documentation of selection criteria and success factors to identify the most promising proposals for funding;

- Provision of the financial industry, research/academia, technologists, entrepreneurs, and the public with a better understanding of the needs and opportunities through outreach programs; and

- Coordination of support for R&D across the financial institutions represented by the FSSCC and its members, providing collaborative review of research proposals and identification of financial institutions interested in participating in the research, providing test data, and deploying results to productive use in the financial industry.

8. Managing and Coordinating SSA Responsibilities

8.1 Program Management Approach

The Assistant Secretary for Financial Institutions is the Treasury official with the responsibility for carrying out the Treasury Department's duties as the SSA for the Banking and Finance Sector. The Department of the Treasury has reviewed the effectiveness of the SSP program to accomplish the SSA responsibilities.

8.2 Processes and Responsibilities

8.2.1 SSP Maintenance and Update

As the SSA, the Treasury Department works with its public and private partners to review and update the SSP in coordination with the review and update cycle of the NIPP. The Treasury Department is the lead coordinator of the review and update cycle. At least twice during each SSP creation cycle, the Treasury Department contacted the FBIIC and the private sector to exchange facts and information that enables the Treasury Department to determine which, if any, parts of the SSP need to be updated or modified based upon changes that have occurred within the sector. Information regarding these changes has been collected, analyzed, and incorporated into the updated SSP. The updated SSP has been circulated to all the FBIIC and private sector members for their individual review and comment. All changes that were made to the updated SSP were forwarded to the designated DHS program office assigned to receive such changes.

8.2.2 SSP Implementation Milestones

The Treasury Department exchanges facts and information with the members of the FBIIC, and the private sector related to the development and update of the Banking and Finance Sector CIKR Protection Annual Report. The Treasury Department provides the updated draft to the appropriate DHS program office. The Sector Annual Report describes progress in reaching milestones in each of the SSP areas.

8.2.3 Resources and Budgets

A majority of the Banking and Finance Sector's assets are privately owned, which allows the private sector to contribute greatly to the sector's investments. The investments include extensive investment in back-up facilities, physical, and IT controls. Many financial organizations have back-up facilities that are geographically dispersed and fully functional in the case of a disruption to their primary sites. Additionally, financial regulators and the private sector invest significant resources in public-private programs, such as exercises and regional partnerships.

Regional partnerships have leveraged non-SSA investment by informing the local financial services industry of credentialing opportunities, communication platforms, and developing relationships with local emergency management resources. Regional partnerships also support each other. For example, ChicagoFIRST, as the "administrator" of RPCfirst, coordinates RPCfirst's annual meetings.

8.2.4 Training and Education

Since the majority of the Banking and Finance Sector is owned and operated by the private sector, the Treasury Department, the FBIIC, and sector participants work together to share the responsibility of protecting the sector. A key component of this responsibility is educating and training public and private sector participants on business continuity, information sharing, emergency response protocols, and the dependence on other sectors. As the owners and operators of the Banking and Finance Sector, the private sector participants are responsible for establishing business continuity and protection programs. The Treasury Department and the other FBIIC members individually assist the private sector in improving sector resilience, as necessary and permissible.

Training efforts are central components of maintaining the financial services sector's resilience before, during, and after an incident. As the SSA, the Treasury Department routinely coordinates communication tests for information sharing between the FBIIC and the private sector to test whether communication protocols are likely to work efficiently and effectively during an incident.

8.3 Implementing the Partnership Model

All of the sector partners must continually work together to promote and maintain the sector partnership model to ensure that the sector is resilient. In the Banking and Finance Sector, the FBIIC serves as the public participants in the sector partnership model at the national level. (See section 1.2 for further details.)

8.4 Information Sharing and Protection

Information sharing is an important aspect of the sector partnership model. In the Banking and Finance Sector, there are a variety of different and complementary information-sharing mechanisms among and between the FBIIC and the private sector. The FBIIC has established emergency response protocols to communicate to the SSA, to each other, and the private sector during an incident. This information-sharing structure enables individuals within the sector to obtain information, as needed.

The Treasury Department has formalized the overall collaboration of the FBIIC and the private sector. As the SSA, the Treasury Department also works with its partners at the Federal level, including DHS, DOJ, and the law enforcement community, to share and analyze sector information. The Treasury Department contacts FBIIC members and the private sector to communicate sector information, as needed. For instance, the Treasury Department and the FDIC each have a detailee at DHS to act as a conduit among DHS, the Treasury Department, and the sector to coordinate information flow regarding critical infrastructure protection issues.

The FS-ISAC is another key component of the Banking and Finance Sector's information-sharing system. On a daily basis, the FS-ISAC reaches more than 11,000 sector participants through partnership with several FSSCC members and promotes information sharing between the public and private sectors. The FS-ISAC provides sector-wide knowledge about physical and cybersecurity risks faced by the financial services sector. The FS-ISAC allows its members to receive threat and vulnerability information immediately; share vulnerabilities and information anonymously and communicate within a secure portal; access new data feeds of threat and vulnerability information; and access a wide range of user data from which users can produce their own reports and metrics.

Appendix A: List of Acronyms and Abbreviations

ACH	Automated Clearing House
ATM	Automated Teller Machine
CFR	Code of Federal Regulations
CFTC	Commodity Futures Trading Commission
CHIPS	The Clearing House Interbank Payments System
CIKR	Critical Infrastructure and Key Resources
CINS	FS-ISAC's Critical Infrastructure Notification System
CME	Chicago Mercantile Exchange
CSBS	Conference of State Bank Supervisors
DHS	Department of Homeland Security
DOJ	Department of Justice
E.O.	Executive Order
FBIIC	Financial and Banking Information Infrastructure Committee
FCA	Farm Credit Administration
FDIC	Federal Deposit Insurance Corporation
FFIEC	Federal Financial Institutions Examination Council
FHFA	Federal Housing Finance Agency
FINRA	Financial Industry Regulatory Authority
FRB	Board of Governors of the Federal Reserve System
FS-ISAC	Financial Services Information Sharing and Analysis Center
FSSCC	Financial Services Sector Coordinating Council for Critical Infrastructure Protection and Homeland Security
FSTC	Financial Services Technology Consortium
GCC	Government Coordinating Council
GDP	Gross Domestic Product
GETS	Government Emergency Telecommunications Service

GSE	Government Sponsored Enterprise
HITRAC	Homeland Infrastructure Threat and Risk Analysis Center
HSPD	Homeland Security Presidential Directive
IP	Office of Infrastructure Protection
ISAC	Information Sharing and Analysis Center
MSRB	Municipal Securities Rulemaking Board
NAIC	National Association of Insurance Commissioners
NASAA	North American Securities Administrators Association
NASCUS	National Association of State Credit Union Supervisors
NCRCG	National Cyber Response Coordination Group
NCS	National Communications System
NCSD	National Cyber Security Division
NCUA	National Credit Union Administration
NFA	National Futures Association
NIPP	National Infrastructure Protection Plan
OCC	Office of Comptroller of the Currency
OTS	Office of Thrift Supervision
PCIS	Partnership for Critical Infrastructure Security
PIN	Personal Identification Number
PWG	President's Working Group on Financial Markets
R&D	Research and Development
RPC	Regional Partnership Council
SCC	Sector Coordinating Council
SEC	Securities and Exchange Commission
SIA	Securities Industry Association
SIAC	Securities Industry Automation Corporation
SIFMA	Securities Information and Financial Markets Association
SIPC	Securities Investor Protection Corporation
SMART	Subject Matter Advisory Response Team
SRO	Self-Regulatory Organization
SSA	Sector-Specific Agency
SSP	Sector-Specific Plan
TIC	Threat and Intelligence Committee
TOPOFF	Top Officials Exercise
TSP	Telecommunications Service Priority

US-CERT	United States Computer Emergency Readiness Team
U.S.S.S.	United States Secret Service
WPS	Wireless Priority Service

Appendix B: Statutory Authorities

Statutory Authorities – Federal Regulators

Commodities Futures Trading Commission

U.S. Code & Regulations	Subject
7 U.S.C. § 1 *et seq.*	Commodity Exchange Act
17 C.F.R. Parts 1-190	Regulations of the CFTC

Farm Credit Administration

U.S. Code & Regulations	Subject
12 U.S.C. § 2001 *et seq.*	The Farm Credit Act of 1971 is the statutory authority to regulate Farm Credit System institutions
12 C.F.R. Parts 600 - 655	Regulations of the FCA

Federal Deposit Insurance Corporation

U.S. Code & Regulations	Subject
12 U.S.C. § 1861 *et seq.*	Bank Service Company Act
12 U.S.C. Ch. 16	Federal Deposit Insurance Corporation

Federal Financial Institutions Examination Council

U.S. Code & Regulations	Subject
12 U.S.C. § 3301 – § 3311	
12 U.S.C. § 3331 -§ 3352	Appraisal Subcommittee

Federal Housing Finance Agency*

Effective July 30, 2008, the Housing and Economic Recovery Act of 2008 (HERA) transferred the supervisory and oversight responsibilities of the Office of Federal Housing Enterprise Oversight (OFHEO) and the Federal Housing Finance Board over the Federal National Mortgage Association (Fannie Mae), Federal Home Loan Mortgage Corporation (Freddie Mac) (the Enterprises), and the Federal Home Loan Banks to a new independent executive branch agency known as the Federal Housing Finance Agency (FHFA). The FHFA is responsible for ensuring that the Enterprises and the Banks operate in a safe and sound manner, including being capitalized adequately, and carry out their public policy missions, including fostering liquid, efficient, competitive, and resilient national housing finance markets. The Enterprises and the Banks continue to operate under regulations promulgated by OFHEO and the FHFB until the FHFA issues its own regulations.

U.S. Code & Regulations	Subject
12 U.S.C. § 1421 *et seq.*	The Federal Home Loan Bank Act principal statute for the Federal Housing Finance Board and Federal Home Loan Banks. **This statute is still in effect, as amended by the Housing and Economic Recovery Act of 2008, P.L. 110-289 (July 30, 2008) (HERA). The new statute is administered by FHFA, rather than the Federal Housing Finance Board.**
12 U.S.C. § 1422a(3)	Duties of the Federal Housing Finance Board is to ensure that the Federal Home Loan Banks operate in a safe and sound manner, and, to the extent consistent with safety and soundness, to supervise the Federal Home Loan Banks, to ensure that the Federal Home Loan Banks carry out their housing finance mission, and to ensure that the Federal Home Loan Banks remain adequately capitalized and able to raise funds in the capital markets. **Repealed by HERA; replaced (as part of the OFHEO statute, below) with provisions establishing new agency, the FHFA.**
12 U.S.C. § 1422b	The general powers of the Federal Housing Finance Board. **Repealed by HERA; replaced (as part of the OFHEO statute, below) with provisions establishing new agency, the FHFA.**
12 C.F.R. Ch. IX	Rules and Regulations of the Federal Housing Finance Board that pertain to the Federal Home Loan Banks. **Still in effect; carried over by § 1312 of HERA until amended or replaced by the FHFA.**
12 C.F.R. Part 985	Most of Federal Housing Finance Board's rules dealing with the Office of Finance. **Still in effect; carried over by § 1312 of HERA until amended or replaced by the FHFA.**

*All of the foregoing regulatory material is still in effect, carried over by § 1312 of HERA until amended or replaced by the FHFA.

Federal Reserve Board

U.S. Code & Regulations	Subject
12 U.S.C. § 248(a)	Federal Reserve Act – Authorizes the Board to examine the accounts, books, and affairs of each member bank.
12 U.S.C. § 1844(c)	Bank Holding Act of 1956 – Authorizes the Board to examine each holding company and subsidiary (except for functionally regulated nonbank subsidiaries, e.g., registered broker dealers and insurance underwriters).
12 U.S.C. § 3105 (c)	International Banking Act of 1978 – Authorizes the Board to examine each branch or agency of a foreign bank.
12 U.S.C. § 611 *et seq.* and 12 C.F.R. § 211.13(b)	Authorize the Board to examine Edge and Agreement corporations.
12 U.S.C. § 1867 (a) and (c)	Bank Service Company Act – Authorizes the Board to examine bank service companies owned by State member insured banks and any independent company that performs the same type of services for a State member insured banks that are authorized under the Bank Service Company Act.

National Credit Union Administration

U.S. Code & Regulations	Subject
12 U.S.C. § 1751 *et seq.*	Federal Credit Union Act – Provides the authority for the National Credit Union Administration to regulate and insure Federally and State chartered credit unions.
12 C.F.R. Parts 700 – 796	National Credit Union Administration Rules & Regulations – Implements the provisions of the Federal Credit Union Act.

Office of Comptroller of the Currency

U.S. Code & Regulations	Subject
12 U.S.C. Ch. 1	Charter
12 U.S.C. Ch. 2	National Banks
12 U.S.C. § 93a	Authorizes the OCC to prescribe rules and regulations for national banks unless such authority is specifically granted to another regulatory agency.
12 U.S.C. § 481	Authorizes the OCC to conduct a thorough examination of national banks and their affiliates and to issue reports of examination.
12 U.S.C. Ch. 18	Bank Service Company Act
12 U.S.C. § 1867	Authorizes the OCC to regulate and examine any bank service company that has a national bank as its principal investor or that provides services to a national bank, or any national bank subsidiary or affiliate that is subject to OCC examination, to the same extent as if such services were being performed by the bank itself on its own premises.
12 U.S.C. §§ 3102, 3108	Authorizes the OCC to approve the creation of one or more branches in a State by a foreign bank and to prescribe such rules, regulations, and orders it considers appropriate to carry out its duties.

Office of Federal Housing Enterprise Oversight*

U.S. Code & Regulations	Subject
12 C.F.R. Ch. XVII	Rules and Regulations of OFHEO pertaining to the Enterprises **Still in effect; carried over by § 1302 of HERA until amended or replaced by the FHFA.**
12 U.S.C. § 4501 et seq.	The Federal Housing Enterprises Financial Safety and Soundness Act of 1992 **Still in effect, as amended by HERA.**
12 U.S.C. § 4511	Establishes the Office of Federal Housing Enterprise Oversight **Replaced by HERA with new section establishing FHFA.**
12 U.S.C. §§ 4512-4526	Duties and Authorities of Director, OFHEO **Amended by HERA with new sections establishing duties and authorities of Director, FHFA.**
12 U.S.C. § 4611 et seq.	Required Capital Levels for Enterprises; Enforcement Powers **Still in effect, as amended by HERA (substantially strengthening the powers of the regulator).**

*All of the foregoing regulatory material is still in effect, carried over by § 1312 of HERA until amended or replaced by the FHFA.

Office of Thrift Supervision

U.S. Code & Regulations	Subject
12 U.S.C. § 1461 *et seq.*	Home Owners' Loan Act – authorizes OTS to examine and supervise Savings Associations and Savings and Loan Holding Companies
12 C.F.R. Parts 500-591	Rules and Regulations of the Office of Thrift Supervision

Securities and Exchange Commission

U.S. Code & Regulations	Subject
15 U.S.C. § 78a *et seq.*	Securities Exchange Act of 1934
15 U.S.C. § 80a-1 *et seq.*	Investment Company Act of 1940
15 U.S.C. § 80b-1 *et seq.*	Investment Advisers Act of 1940
17 CFR Part 240	Securities Exchange Act of 1934
17 CFR Part 242	Securities Exchange Act of 1934

Securities Investor Protection Corporation*

U.S. Code & Regulations	Subject
15 U.S.C. § 78aaa *et seq.*	The Securities Investor Protection Act of 1970
15 U.S.C. § 78ccc(e)(2)	Rules to effectuate the purpose and operations of SIPC. See 17 C.F.R. Part 300
15 U.S.C. § 78fff(b)	Shall allow SIPC to conduct a liquidation proceeding "in accordance with, and as though it were being conducted under chapters 1,3, and 5 and subchapters I and II of chapter 7" of the Bankruptcy Code, 11 U.S.C. § 101 *et seq.*

* This corporation is neither a Federal nor State regulator; however, it was established by a Federal statute.

Department of the Treasury

U.S. Code & Regulations	Subject
12 U.S.C. § 90	National Banks Depositories of Public Money & Financial Agents
31 U.S.C. § 3101	Public Debt Limit
31 U.S.C. § 3102	Bonds
31 U.S.C. § 3104	Certificates of Indebtedness and Treasury Bills
31 U.S.C. § 3103	Notes
31 U.S.C. § 3105	Savings Bonds
31 U.S.C. § 3121	Procedure
31 U.S.C. § 3122	Banks and trust companies as depositories
31 U.S.C. § 3123	Payment of obligations and interest on the public debt
15 U.S.C. § 78o-5	Government securities brokers and dealers

Statutory Authorities – State Regulators

Conference of State Bank Supervisors – State Banking Departments

State	Banking Law/Statute
Alabama	Alabama Banking Code Title 5, Chapters 1A through 13B and Chapter 20
Alaska	Alaska Statutes (AS) Title 06 – Banks and Financial Institutions
Arizona	Arizona Revised Statutes (ARS) Title 6 – Banks and Financial Institutions
Arkansas	Arkansas Code Title 23, Subtitle 2 – Financial Institutions and Securities
California	California Financial Code Divisions 1, 2, 5, 7 and 16 – Banks and Trust Companies (Division 1), Savings Associations (Division 2), Credit Unions (Division 5), Industrial Loan Companies and Premium Finance Companies (Division 7), Issuers of Money Orders (Division 16)
Colorado	Colorado Revised Statutes (CRS) Title 11 – Financial Institutions
Connecticut	The Banking Law of Connecticut – Title 36a
Delaware	Delaware Code Title 5 – Banking
District of Columbia	District of Columbia Official Code Title 26 – Banks and Other Financial Institutions

State	Banking Law/Statute
Florida	Florida Statutes Title XXXVIII, Chapters 655 – 667: Banks and Banking
Georgia	Official Code of Georgia Annotated (OCGA) Title 7 – Financial Institutions Code of Georgia
Guam	Title 11, Guam Code Annotated (GCA) – Finance & Taxation, Chapter 106 – Banks
Hawaii	Hawaii Revised Statutes (HRS) Chapter 412 – Code of Financial Institutions
Idaho	Idaho Statutes Title 26 – Banks and Banking
Illinois	Illinois Compiled Statutes (ILCS) Chapter 205 – Financial Regulation
Indiana	Indiana Code (IC) Title 28 – Financial Institutions
Iowa	Iowa Code Chapter 524 – Iowa Banking Act
Kansas	Kansas Statutes Annotated (K.S.A.) Chapter 9 – Banking Code
Kentucky	Kentucky Revised Statutes (KRS) Chapter 287 – Banks and Trust Companies
Louisiana	Louisiana Revised Statutes (R.S.) Title 6 – Banks and Banking
Maine	Maine Revised Statutes (M.R.S.A.) Title 9-B – Financial Institutions; also called the Maine Banking Code
Maryland	Maryland Annotated Code – Financial Institutions
Massachusetts	General Laws of Massachusetts Part I, Title XXII, Chapters 167 – 174
Michigan	Michigan Compiled Law (MCL) Chapter 487 – Financial Institutions
Minnesota	Minnesota Statutes 2005 Chapters 46 – 59 – Banking
Mississippi	Mississippi Code of 1972, Annotated – Title 81 – Banks & Financial Institutions
Missouri	Missouri Revised Statutes Title XXIV – Business and Financial Institutions
Montana	Montana Code Annotated 2005 Title 32 – Financial Institutions
Nebraska	Nebraska Revised Statutes Chapter 8 – Banks and Banking
Nevada	Nevada Revised Statutes (NRS) Title 55 – Banks and Related Organizations
New Hampshire	New Hampshire Revised Statutes Annotated (NH RSA) Title XXXV – Banks and Banking; Loan Associations; Credit Unions
New Jersey	New Jersey Statutes Annotated (N.J.S.A.) Title 17 – Corporations and Institutions for Finance and Insurance
New Mexico	New Mexico Statutes Annotated 1978 (NMSA 1978) Chapter 58 – Financial Institutions and Regulations

State	Banking Law/Statute
New York	New York Banking Laws (NYBL)
North Carolina	North Carolina General Statutes (GS) Chapter 53 – Banks
North Dakota	North Dakota Century Code (NDCC) Title 6 – Banks and Banking
Ohio	Ohio Revised Code (ORS) Title XI – Financial Institutions
Oklahoma	Oklahoma Statutes (O.S.) Title 6 – Banks and Trust Companies
Oregon	Oregon Revised Statutes (ORS) Title 53 – Financial Institutions
Pennsylvania	Pennsylvania Banking Code of 1965 - Unconsolidated Pennsylvania Statutes Title 7 – Banks and Banking
Puerto Rico	Laws of Puerto Rico Annotated (L.P.R.A.) Title 7 – Banking
Rhode Island	Rhode Island General Laws (R.I.G.L.) Title 19 – Financial Institutions
South Carolina	South Carolina Code of Laws Title 34 - Banking, Financial Institutions and Money
South Dakota	South Dakota Codified Laws Title 51A – Banks and Banking
Tennessee	Tennessee Code Annotated (T.C.A.) Title 45 – Banks and Financial Institutions
Texas	Texas Finance Code (TFC) Title 3 – Financial Institutions and Businesses
Utah	Utah Code Annotated (UCA) Title 7 – Financial Institutions Act
Vermont	Vermont Statutes Annotated (VSA) Title 8 – Banking and Insurance
Virgin Islands	Virgin Islands Code Title 9
Virginia	Code of Virginia Title 6.1 – Banking and Finance
Washington	Revised Code of Washington (RCW)
West Virginia	West Virginia Code Chapter 31A – Banks and Banking; Chapter 31C – Credit Unions; Chapter 46A, Article 4 – Regulated Consumer Lenders; Chapter 31, Article 17 – Residential Mortgage Lender, Broker and Servicer Act; Chapter 32A, Article 2 – Checks and Money Order Sales, Money Transmission Services, Transportation and Currency Exchange; Chapter 32A, Article 3 – Check Cashing
Wisconsin	Wisconsin Statutes Chapter 138 - Money and Rates of Interest; Chapter 214 – Savings Banks; Chapter 215 – Savings & Loans Associations; Chapter 220 – Banking; Chapter 221 – State Banks; Chapter 222 – Universal Banks; Chapter 223 – Trust Company Banks & Other Fiduciaries; Chapter 224 – Miscellaneous Banking and Financial Institutions Provisions; Chapter 428 – First Lien Real Estate Loans
Wyoming	Wyoming Statutes (W.S.) Title 13 – Banks, Banking and Finance

Below is a listing of the State statutory citations that form the basis for the regulation and taxation of the business of insurance. It should be noted that State laws often authorize State insurance regulators to publish regulations necessary to carry out the laws regulating insurers, insurance producers, and other regulated entities. Citations to these regulations are not included for brevity. Insurance regulators also inform regulated entities about regulatory matters through the issuance of bulletins, guidelines, or other informative communications. These documents are also not cited because of size limitations.

Code & Regulations	State	URL
§§ 27-1-1 to 27-57-6	AL	http://www.aldoi.gov/Legal/Title27.html
§§ 21.06.010 to 21.90.910	AK	http://www.legis.state.ak.us/cgi-bin/folioisa.dll/stattx05/query=*/doc/{t9131}
§§ 20-101 to 20-3155	AZ	http://www.azleg.state.az.us/ArizonaRevisedStatutes.asp?Title=20
§§ 23-60-101 to 23-103-316	AR	http://www.arkleg.state.ar.us/NXT/gateway.dll?f=templates&fn=default.htm&vid=blr:code Click on "+" for Arkansas Code, then click "+" for Title 23, Subtitle 3 to view/obtain entire code.
Ins. §§ 1 to 16030	CA	http://www.leginfo.ca.gov/.html/ins_table_of_contents.html
Title 10 Insurance §§ 10-1-101 to 10-20-120 §§10-21-101 to 10-21-106 Repealed in 2004 (Colorado Health Care Coverage Act)	CO	http://198.187.128.12/colorado/lpext.dll?f=templates&fn=fs-main.htm&2.0 Open Statutes, click on Title 10 Insurance folder to view/obtain entire code.
§§ 38a-1 to 38a-1050	CT	http://www.cga.ct.gov/2005/pub/Title38a.htm?cidNav=|
Tit. 18 §§ 101 to 8014	DE	http://www.delcode.state.de.us/title18/index.htm#TopOfPage
§§ 31-101 to 31-5608.04	DC	http://198.187.128.12/dc/lpext.dll?=templates&fn=fs-main.htm&2.0 Open Division V Local Business Affairs, click on Title 31 Insurance and Securities to view/obtain code.
§§ 624.01 to 651.134	FL	http://www.flsenate.gov/Statutes/index.cfm?App_mode=Display_Index&Title_Request=XXXVII#TitleXXXVII
§§ 33-1-1 to 33-61-2	GA	http://www.legis.ga.gov/legis/GaCode/?title=33
§§ 431:1-100 to 431:30-124	HI	http://www.capitol.hawaii.gov/hrscurrent/vol09_ch0431-0435e/hrs0431/hrs_0431-.htm This link is to a list. Click on "Next" to view individual statutes. http://www.hawaii.gov/dcca/areas/ins/main/hrs/ - Listing of statutes pertaining to insurance

Code & Regulations	State	URL
§§ 41-101 to 41-5702	ID	http://www3.state.id.us/idstat/TOC/41FTOC.html
215 ILCS 5/1 to 215 ILCS 165/30	IL	http://www.ilga.gov/legislation/ilcs/ilcs5.asp?ActID=1249&ChapAct=215%26nbsp%3BILCS%26nbsp%3B5%2F&ChapterID=22&ChapterName=INSURANCE&ActName=Illinois+Insurance+Code%2E
IC 27-1-1-1 to 27-17-14-2	IN	http://www.in.gov/legislative/ic/code/title27/
§§ 505.1 to 523I.814	IA	http://coolice.legis.state.ia.us/Cool-ICE/default.asp?category=billinfo&service=IowaCode Type 505 to begin viewing statutes.
§§ 40-101 to 40-5301	KS	http://www.kslegislature.org/legsrv-statutes/articlesList.do Under Statute Table of Contents, click on Chapter 40 Insurance.
§§ 304.1-010 to 304.99-152	KY	http://www.lrc.ky.gov/KRS/304-01/CHAPTER.HTM Will need to click on "next chapter" to continue viewing.
R.S. §§ 22:1 to 22:3205	LA	http://www.legis.state.la.us/lss/lss.asp?folder=1 Click on Title 22 Insurance.
Tit. 24-A §§ 1 to 6971 Tit. 24 §§ 1 to 3307	ME	http://janus.state.me.us/legis/statutes/24-A/title24-Ach0sec0.html http://janus.state.me.us/legis/statutes/24/title24ch0sec0.html
Ins. §§ 1-101 to 29-102	MD	http://www.dsd.state.md.us/comar/Annot_Code_Idx/InsuranceIndex.htm
§§ 175:1 to 175:225; §§ 175A:1 to 175K:16	MA	http://www.mass.gov/legis/laws/mgl/gl-175-toc.htm
§§ 500.100 to 500.8302 §§ 550.1 to 550.2009	MI	http://www.legislature.mi.gov/(S(gn34nh45ga0dggjhhil4ll45))/mileg.aspx?page=getObject&objectName=mcl-Act-218-of-1956 http://www.legislature.mi.gov/(S(gn34nh45ga0dggjhhil4ll45))/mileg.aspx?page=getobject&objectname=mcl-chap550
§§ 59A.01 to79A.32	MN	http://ros.leg.mn/stats/59A.html
§§ 83-1-1 to 83-67-5	MS	http://198.187.128.12/mississippi/lpext.dll?f=templates&fn=fs-main.htm&2.0 Click on Code, then "more" to locate Title 83 Insurance.
§§ 374.010 to 385.080	MO	http://www.moga.mo.gov/statutes/chapters/chap374.htm http://www.moga.mo.gov/STATUTES/STATUTES.HTM
§§ 33-1-101 to 33-38-108	MT	http://data.opi.state.mt.us/bills/mca_toc/33.htm
§§ 44-101 to 44.8107	NE	http://uniweb.legislature.ne.gov/legaldocs/search.php Scroll down to "View All" and select 44-Insurance from drop down.

Code & Regulations	State	URL
§§ 679A.010 to 697.370	NV	http://www.leg.state.nv.us/NRS/NRS-679A.html http://www.leg.state.nv.us/NRS/Index.cfm
§§ 400-A:1 to 420-K:7	NH	http://www.gencourt.state.nh.us/rsa/html/NHTOC/NHTOC-XXXVII.htm
§§ 17:1-1 to 17B:36-4	NJ	http://lis.njleg.state.nj.us/cgi-bin/om_isapi.dll?clientID=57988753&Depth=2&depth=2&expandheadings=on&headingswithhits=on&hitsperheading=on&infobase=statutes.nfo&record={52AB}&softpage=Doc_Frame_PG42
§§ 59A-1-1 to 59A-59-4	NM	http://www.conwaygreene.com/nmsu/lpext.dll?f=templates&fn=main-h.htm&2.0 Open folder, New Mexico Statutes and Court, then click on Statutory Chapters in N.M. Statutes, then select 59A. Insurance Code.
Ins. Law §§ 101 to 9901	NY	http://www.ins.state.ny.us/regclinx.htm Scroll down to New York State Consolidated Laws – Insurance link and follow directions to open link.
§§ 58-1-1 to 58-91-80	NC	http://www.ncga.state.nc.us/EnactedLegislation/Statutes/HTML/ByChapter/Chapter_58.html
§§ 26.1-01-01 to 26.1-53-09	ND	http://www.legis.nd.gov/cencode/t261.html
§§ 3901.01 to 3999.99	OH	http://onlinedocs.andersonpublishing.com/oh/lpExt.dll?f=templates&fn=main-h.htm&cp=PORC Scroll down to Title XXXIX Insurance.
36 §§ 101 to 7004	OK	http://www.oscn.net/applications/oscn/index.asp?level=1&ftdb=STOKST36&level=1
§§ 731.004 to 752.055	OR	http://www.oregoninsurance.org/lawsrules.html Click on Insurance Laws of Oregon 2005 link.
§§ 40-1-011 to 40-6335	PA	http://members.aol.com/DKM1/40.html
tit. 26 §§ 101 to 8061	PR	www.michie.com Select Jurisdiction of Puerto Rico, will need to obtain a free password/id to access Puerto Rico's code.
§§ 27-1-1 to 27-69-6	RI	http://www.rilin.state.ri.us/Statutes/TITLE27/INDEX.HTM
§§ 38-1-10 to 38-93-60	SC	http://www.scstatehouse.net/code/titl38.htm
§§ 58-1-1 to 58-46-26	SD	http://legis.state.sd.us/statutes/DisplayStatute.aspx?Type=Statute&Statute=58

Code & Regulations	State	URL
§§ 56-1-101 to 56-57-106	TN	http://198.187.128.12/tennessee/lpext.dll?f=templates&fn=fs-main.htm&2.0 Open Tennessee Code, open "more" then select Title 56 Insurance.
I.C. Art. 1.01 to 29.14; Ins. §§ 30.001 to 5001.002	TX	http://tlo2.tlc.state.tx.us/statutes/in.toc.htm
§§ 31A-1-101 to 31A-39-101	UT	http://www.le.state.ut.us/~code/TITLE31A/TITLE31A.htm
tit. 8 §§ 3301 to 8517	VT	http://www.leg.state.vt.us/statutes/chapters.cfm?Title=08
Title 22 §§ 1 to 1728	VI	http://198.187.128.12/virginislands/lpext.dll?f=templates&fn=fs-main.htm&2.0 Open V.I. Code, open "more" then select Title 22 Insurance.
§§ 38.2-100 to 38.2-6201	VA	http://leg1.state.va.us/000/reg/TOC14005.HTM
§§ 48.01.010 to 48.140.080	WA	http://apps.leg.wa.gov/rcw/default.aspx?Cite=48
§§ 33-1-1 to 33-48-12	WV	http://www.legis.state.wv.us/WVCODE/33/masterfrmFrm.htm
§§ 600.01 to 655.68	WI	http://www.legis.state.wi.us/rsb/Statutes.html Scroll down to Insurance.
§§ 26-1-101 to 26-50-109	WY	http://legisweb.state.wy.us/statutes/statutes.aspx?file=titles/Title26/Title26.htm

North American Securities Administrators Association

State	Statute
Alabama	Al. Code 1975, §§ 8-6-1 to 8-6-33
Alaska	Ak. St. §§ 45.55.010 to 45.55.955
Arizona	A.R.S. §§ 44-1801 to 44-2126
Arkansas	A.C.A. §§ 23-42-101 to 23-42-509
California	CA CORP §§ 25000 to 25707
Colorado	CO ST §§11-51-101 to 11-51-908
Connecticut	CT ST §§ 36b-2 to 36b-33

State	Statute
Delaware	6 Del.C. §§ 7301 to 7330
District of Columbia	DC ST §§ 31-5601.01 to 31-5608.04
Florida	FL ST §§ 517.011 to 517.32
Georgia	GA ST §§ 10-5-1 to 10-5-24
Hawaii	HI ST §§ 485-1 to 485-25
Idaho	ID ST §§ 30-14-101 to 30-14-703
Illinois	815 ILCS §§ 5/1 to 5/19
Indiana	IN ST §§ 23-2-1-27
Iowa	IA ST §§ 502.101 to 502.701
Kansas	KS ST §§ 17-12a101 to 17-12a703
Kentucky	KY ST §§ 292.310 to 292.550, 292.991
Louisiana	LA. R.S. §§ 701 to 724
Maine	32 M.R.S.A. §§ 16101 to 16702
Maryland	MD Code, Corporations and Associations, §§ 11-101 to 11-805
Massachusetts	M.G.L.A. c. 110A, §§ 101 to 417
Michigan	MI ST §§ 451.501 to 451.818
Minnesota	MN ST §§ 80A.01 to 80A.31
Mississippi	MS Code 1972, §§ 75-71-101 to 75-71-735
Missouri	V.A.M.S. §§ 409.1-101 to 409.7-703
Montana	MCA §§ 30-10-101 to 30-10-308
Nebraska	NE ST §§ 8-1101 to 8-1123
Nevada	NV ST §§ 90.211 to 90.860
New Hampshire	NH ST §§ 421-B:1 to 421-B:34
New Jersey	NJ ST §§ 49:3-47 to 49:3-76
New Mexico	N.M.S.A §§ 46-8-1 to 46-8-10

State	Statute
New York	NY ST §§ 352 to 359-h
North Carolina	NC ST §§ 78A-1 to 78A-66
North Dakota	NDCC §§ 10-04-01 to 10-04-20
Ohio	OH ST §§ 1707.01 to 1707.99
Oklahoma	OK ST T. 71 §§ 1-101 to 1-701
Oregon	OR ST §§ 59.005 to 59.451, 59.991, 59.995
Pennsylvania	70 P.S. §§ 1-101 to 1-704
Puerto Rico	10 L.P.R.A. §§ 851 to 895
Rhode Island	RI ST 7-11-101 to 7-11-806
South Carolina	SC Code 1976, §§ 35-1-101 to 35-1-703
South Dakota	SDCL §§ 47-31B-101 to 47-31B-703
Tennessee	TN ST. §§ 48-2-101 to 48-2-117
Texas	TX CIV ST ART 581-1 to 581-60a
Utah	UT ST § 61-1-1 to 61-1-30
Vermont	VT ST T.9 §§ 5101 to 5612
Virginia	Va. Code 1950, §§ 13.1-501 to 13.1-527.3
Washington	RCWA §§ 21.20.005 to 21.20.940
West Virginia	W. Va. Code §§ 32-1-101 to 32-1-418
Wisconsin	WI ST §§ 551.01 to 551.67
Wyoming	WY ST §§ 17-4-101 to 17-4-131

Guidance & Key Documents – Federal Regulators

Federal Financial Institution Examination Council (FFIEC)

The FFIEC is a formal interagency body empowered to prescribe uniform principles, standards, and report forms for the Federal examination of financial institutions by the Board of Governors of the Federal Reserve System, the Federal Deposit Insurance Corporation, the National Credit Union Administration, the Office of the Comptroller of the Currency, and the Office of Thrift Supervision. FFIEC guidance documents are issued by each aforementioned agency and are available through the agencies web sites. However, the FFIEC-developed IT Handbooks are available at **www.ffiec.gov/ffiecinfobase**.

Federal Deposit Insurance Corporation

FDIC industry guidance documents are issued as Financial Institution Letters and Special Alerts. These documents are available at **http://www.fdic.gov/news/news/financial/2009/index.html**.

Federal Reserve Board

Federal Reserve Board industry guidance documents are issued as Supervision and Regulation Letters and may be found at **http://www.federalreserve.gov/boarddocs/srletters**.

National Credit Union Administration

NCUA industry guidance documents are issued in the form of Letters to Credit Unions and may be found at **http://www.ncua.gov/resources/letterscreditunion.aspx**.

Office of the Comptroller of the Currency

OCC industry guidance documents are issued as OCC Bulletins or Bank Bulletins. These documents are available at **http://www.occ.gov/issue.htm**.

Office of Thrift Supervision

OTS industry guidance documents are issued as Thrift Bulletins and they are available at **http://www.ots.gov/?p=ThriftBulletins**.

Federal Housing Finance Agency

FHFA issues FHFA Agency Guidance papers which are available at **http://www.fhfa.gov/Default.aspx?Page=94**.

Bank for International Settlement

The Bank for International Settlement's Basel Committee on Banking Supervision has issued various publications which may be found at **http://www.bis.org/bcbs**.

Guidance & Key Documents – State Regulators

Conference of State Bank Supervisors

Title	URL
Nationwide State-Federal Supervisory Agreement	http://www.csbs.org/Content/NavigationMenu/RegulatoryAffairs/ SupervisoryAgreementsApplications/nationwide_state_fed_supervisory_agrmnt.pdf
Nationwide Cooperative Agreement	http://www.csbs.org/Content/NavigationMenu/RegulatoryAffairs/ SupervisoryAgreementsApplications/nationwide_coop_agrmnt.pdf
Nationwide State Foreign Bank Office (FBO) Agreement	http://www.csbs.org/Content/NavigationMenu/RegulatoryAffairs/ SupervisoryAgreementsApplications/state_fbo_agrmnt.pdf
Nationwide State-Federal Foreign Bank Office (FBO) Agreement	http://www.csbs.org/Content/NavigationMenu/RegulatoryAffairs/ SupervisoryAgreementsApplications/state_federal_fbo_agrmnt.pdf
Nationwide Cooperative Agreement for the Supervision and Examination of Multi-State Trust Institutions (Nationwide Trust Agreement)	http://www.csbs.org/Content/NavigationMenu/RegulatoryAffairs/ SupervisoryAgreementsApplications/nationwide_agrmnt_multi-state_trust_op.pdf
CSBS Statutory Options for Multi-State Trust Activities	http://www.csbs.org/Content/NavigationMenu/RegulatoryAffairs/ SupervisoryAgreementsApplications/model_trust_law.pdf
State/Federal Supervisory Protocol	http://www.csbs.org/Content/NavigationMenu/RegulatoryAffairs/ SupervisoryAgreementsApplications/StateFederalSupervisoryProtocol.pdf

National Association of State Credit Union Supervisors

Title	URL
Nationwide Cooperative Interstate Branching Agreement for the Supervision of State-Chartered Credit Unions	http://www.nascus.org/publications/Interstate_Branch_Agree.pdf
NASCUS/State Regulators and NCUA Document of Cooperation	http://www.nascus.org/pdf/DOC2007.pdf

Appendix C: 2008 FSSCC R&D Agenda

Financial Services Sector Coordinating Council
for Critical Infrastructure Protection
and Homeland Security

Research and Development Committee

Research Agenda for the Banking and Finance Sector

September 2008

Overview

The Financial Services Sector Coordinating Council for Critical Infrastructure Protection and Homeland Security (FSSCC) supports research and development initiatives to protect the physical and electronic infrastructure of the Banking and Finance Sector, and to protect its customers by enhancing the Sector's resilience and integrity.[26] The FSSCC established the Research and Development Committee ("R&D Committee") in 2004 as a standing committee to identify priorities for research, promote development initiatives to significantly improve the resilience of the Financial Services Sector, engage stakeholders (including academic institutions and government agencies), and coordinate these activities on behalf of the Banking and Finance Sector.[27] This research agenda is intended as a "living" document and has been updated to reflect advances in technology and the changing threat environment. The R&D Committee revised the priorities paper in early 2008 by consolidating nine research and development challenges into seven, re-evaluating the priority order, and seeking input from experts in academia, government, financial services and information technology communities.[28]

The R&D Committee believes that much of the financial sector's R&D needs are unique to the Banking and Finance Sector. However, the Committee believes other critical infrastructure sectors would also benefit from investments in R&D directed at the financial services industry. The FSSCC R&D Committee is working with the Treasury and Department of Homeland Security to identify funding mechanisms to address the priorities identified by the FSSCC. Treasury and Homeland Security are working with the financial sector, academia, and other government agencies to focus on cyber security concerns.

The information security industry has grown rapidly to mitigate risks by providing a myriad of products and services, including firewalls, access controls, anti-virus and anti-spyware programs, audits, standards (e.g., Common Criteria), and software patches. Financial institutions have responded by establishing governance models that include chief information security officers who manage information security risks by applying the appropriate mix of technology, processes, and expertise to safeguard data and information systems. Ongoing research and development is vital to supplement these advances, and to securing the economic well-being of the United States.

---

[26] The FSSCC is a private sector organization of more than 45 financial sector association and financial institutions representing all of the financial associations and major operators. The FSSCC was created in 2002 to work with US government on matters related to the National Response Framework (NRF). As per the NRF, the designated agency on the government side of this communication is the U.S. Department of Treasury (Treasury). Treasury is also responsible for coordinating the financial services sector's contribution to the NRF, or the "sector-specific plan." The NRF requires that all sectors include Research & Development efforts in their sector-specific plans. To this end, the FSSCC created an R&D Committee in 2004. The mission of the FSSCC R&D Committee is to support research and development initiatives to ensure the protection and resilience of the physical and electronic infrastructure of Banking and Finance activities that are vital to the nation's economic well-being. More information on the FSSCC is available at **http://www.fsscc.org**.

[27] Appendix A provides a list of current R&D Committee members.

[28] The 2006 version of the Challenges is based on a paper entitled *Closing the Gap: A Research and Development Agenda to Improve the Resilience of the Financial and Banking Sector*, by Dr. Jerrold M. Grochow of the MITRE Corporation and the Massachusetts Institute of Technology, with the support of officials from the U.S. Department of the Treasury, Office of Critical Infrastructure Protection and Compliance Policy. In updating the paper, the R&D Committee received very positive comments on the draft from experts from academia, government and the technology and financial services communities in terms of the paper's depth and breath. Reviewers suggested that the Committee narrow the list of priorities, list more specific R&D projects that have clear independent and dependent variables, focus on risk measurement and how R&D outcomes would result in risk reduction, and include more examples to explain why projects are important to the banking and finance sector.

Discussions with academic institutions, however, reveal funding is very limited to conduct priority research. Financial institutions are battling new and constantly changing threats with old technologies and processes. Nevertheless, the Banking and Finance Sector is capable of coordinating research and programs to address its priorities. Coordination would drive efficiencies and help direct available research investments. Therefore, increasing and sustaining funding levels for R&D is critical. This might be possible by using a translational research model that partners researchers with stakeholders, has clear goals, a mechanism of technology transfer that includes intellectual property ownership resolution, and metrics to gauge the effectiveness of the R&D solutions.

The R&D Committee has identified four major gaps in financial sector R&D:

- Greater transparency is needed to make key stakeholders (financial institutions, academia and government) aware of each other's R&D efforts and needs.

- Better coordination is needed to facilitate activities among stakeholders in the US, as well as coordination with international organizations, subject to legal and regulatory restrictions and national security interests. Better coordination would drive efficiencies, help direct available research investments, and help achieve common goals more effectively.

- Academics seek access to sensitive data of financial institutions. However, access to data is a major concern for financial institutions. In general, financial institutions are reluctant to provide data given the sensitivity of data and the potential for misuse.

- Funding for R&D by the federal government and private sector is inadequate to meet the critical needs of the Banking and Finance Sector. Additional funding is necessary to meet current and emerging challenges.

In response to several of these gaps, in 2007 the FSSCC established a program to connect experts within the Banking and Finance Sector with researchers in academia: the Subject Matter Advisory Response Team (SMART) Program. The program assists research and development organizations working on critical infrastructure protection projects by providing subject matter expertise from financial institutions necessary to facilitate their research and development endeavors.

The committee has identified seven priority areas for R&D. Each of these seven challenges is important, but this should not be considered an all-inclusive list. The Committee has ranked these in order of importance recognizing that there are divergent views as to the appropriate order.

Executive Summary

The following are the top priorities of the Research and Development Committee of the Financial Services Sector Coordinating Council for Critical Infrastructure Protection and Homeland Security.

<u>Advancing the State of the Art in Designing and Testing Secure Applications</u>. Software applications are complex and often insecure and thus introduce vulnerabilities. Historically, acquisition requirements have favored functionality over security which has led to a state of software development that often does not emphasize security. Financial institutions have begun demanding more secure application development. Because financial institutions often cannot be sure that their applications are secure, they must develop and implement costly and inefficient compensating controls. Financial institutions need a robust, effective, affordable, and timely security testing methodology, and practice to gain the confidence required to deploy application software into sometimes-hostile environments for purposes of practical and appropriate risk management. Research is needed to develop effective procurement standards, software developer education, and testing guidelines. In addition, research is needed to develop tools for producing, measuring and testing secure application software.

<u>More Secure and Resilient Financial Transaction Systems</u>. The Financial Services industry is dependent upon information technology infrastructure, much of which is owned and operated by third parties outside the financial services industry. This infrastructure is constantly under attack by hackers and identity thieves who seek to exploit vulnerabilities in networks, devices and applications for financial gain. Research is needed to better understand these threats, improve the security and resilience of the financial transaction infrastructure, enhance the protections available to prevent the increasingly common downloads of malware by criminal elements that bypass existing defenses such as anti-virus and anti-spyware, and to develop metrics to evaluate the resilience of the information technology infrastructure.

<u>Enrollment and Identity Credential Management</u>. The financial services industry depends on the ability of financial institutions to identify, authenticate and authorize activity by customers before the customers access information and undertake transactions through remote channels where direct human interaction is not possible. Inadequate controls can leave financial institutions and their customers vulnerable to attacks. Research is needed to study how to make the identity management process better and less susceptible to social engineering attacks.

<u>Understanding the Human Insider Threat</u>. Financial institutions must trust employees who have access to sensitive personal and financial information. Current strategies for identifying trustworthy candidates rely upon historical methods such as background and credit history checks as well as identity confirmation. Such methods often do not sufficiently identify insider-fraud perpetrators ahead of time and can be costly to maintain. Research is needed to develop holistic solutions to the insider-authentication problem, including the development of a data frame to predict the likelihood of insider attacks based on differing scenarios, or the development of continuous, unobtrusive monitoring to reduce the risks posed by insiders.

Data Centric Protection Strategies. To maintain trust and the integrity of data, financial institutions must protect sensitive data but also share it with third parties, such as merchants and processors. Increasingly, devices and networks are vulnerable to malicious code or data breaches. Research is needed to develop secure data file and document tagging technologies to classify information, and to enforce rules on access so that sensitive information is protected as intended by its original owner, regardless of where it traverses.

Better Measures of the Value of Security Investments. Traditionally, investment decisions surrounding security implementations have followed a "Return on Investment" (ROI) decision making process. The ROI model does not always fit well into the security space because it can be difficult to quantify hypothetical losses averted through increased security. The creation of cost-benefit models for security spending might be more appropriate because they would take into account intangible benefits such as increased customer confidence and decreased brand exposure. Research is needed to quantify the costs and benefits of security investments using models that are understood by financial risk managers.

Development of Practical Standards. The financial services industry relies on numerous standards and practices but has not succeeded in developing quantifiable measures for how these standards and practices reduce risk and enhance resilience of critical infrastructures. Research is needed to measure the impact of standards and practices.

Table of Contents

Challenge 1: Advancing the State of the Art in Designing and Testing Secure Applications

The Situation

Information technology vulnerabilities emanate from two primary sources: (1) software flaws, and (2) inadequate patching and configuration practice—and therefore require two different threads of thinking about research. Across the entire financial services industry, the information protection and risk management community is generally not well equipped to accurately or completely define, specify, estimate, calculate, and measure how to design and test secure application software. Although continued mitigations against network vulnerabilities remain important, an increasing number of attacks are against software applications. However, financial institutions typically spend more to mitigate network vulnerabilities than software application vulnerabilities. Business requirements and risk assessments should drive resource allocations. Risks are driven by complex applications developed in-house and by partners, extension of powerful business applications to vulnerable customers, and increasingly organized criminal attacks (e.g., SQL injections to steal copies of data bases, cross-site scripting). To be effective, application security strategies must incorporate development standards and training, automated and manual code reviews, and penetration testing with and without design specifications or source code of the applications being tested. Some financial regulators have issued supervisory guidance on risks associated with web-based applications, urging banks to focus adequate attention on these risks and appropriate risk management practices.[29]

The testing of financial institution applications for security vulnerabilities stemming from software flaws is often inadequate, incomplete, or non-existent. Whether commercial off-the-shelf (COTS) applications are used stand-alone or integrated into custom-built applications, financial institutions cannot gain the confidence that is needed to deploy business-critical software without some proof of evaluation for obvious application security flaws (e.g., un-validated user input, buffer-overrun conditions). Without this confidence, financial institutions are forced to develop countermeasures and compensating controls to counter these unknown potential threats and undocumented features of the software. While functional testing by development teams and outside software developers is necessary, it is insufficient without explicit security assurance testing and corresponding evidence of testing results. Financial institutions need a robust, effective, affordable, and timely security testing methodology and practice to gain the confidence required to deploy application software into sometimes hostile environments for purposes of practical and appropriate risk management.

To minimize vulnerability, financial institutions have urged major software providers to improve the quality of their software development and testing processes for utility software, such as operating systems, but are only beginning to urge application software developers to do the same. Major software companies and outsourcing providers are responding by developing more secure code. However, while these are important and worthwhile efforts, the financial services industry (and other users of

---

[29] See OCC Bulletin 2008-16 Guidance on Application Security ([29] See OCC Bulletin 2008-16 Guidance on Application Security (**http://www.occ.treas.gov/ftp/bulletin/2008-16.html**).).

software) remains at risk from fundamental software development practices that produce vulnerable software in the very beginning stages of development. This vulnerable software has, in turn, resulted in substantial increase in application-level attacks. Risk managers in financial institutions continue to look for solutions.

The financial services industry needs research on how to specify, design, and implement secure software and measure its associated lifecycle costs and the benefits of the various information security technologies and processes. The industry would benefit from better understanding of how to develop, test, and measure secure application software.

Impact and Consequences

The cost to the industry of maintaining, upgrading, and patching software has grown to the point that it is impeding the ability of the industry to add needed new functionality. In the short run, software flaws are fixed via patches, but in the long run, better coding practices will reduce the number of flaws. However, the inability to keep abreast with the growing vulnerabilities of application software and to keep up with remediating these vulnerabilities is leading to an increase in the likelihood of catastrophic failures, unacceptable service disruptions, and highly publicized losses due to fraud, errors, and misuse of data.

Cyber security breaches are a risk in today's interconnected world with its ever expanding flow of data. The financial and business impact of unauthorized intrusions can be damaging. Financial institutions experience a continuing onslaught of malware, Trojans, worms, viruses, spyware, and the resulting fraud and loss of privacy, in addition to the fear of malicious cyber attacks that can disrupt or preclude access to a web service. Every day, an organization's information system is at risk of attack from insecure software applications. And while many of these attacks are little more than harmless pranks, other more insidious assaults can wreak significant economic and operational damage.

Desired Functionality

A clear and accepted methodology to design, implement, measure and test application software to assure that application software is secure from attack and hack. This would include the ability to:

Provide software security testing and certification methodologies and standards that are relevant and immediately useful to the financial industry. The results of this research should:

- Evaluate the commercial effectiveness of existing software security certification and testing programs (e.g., Common Criteria).

- Explore more effective ways to design, test, and measure software during its development to minimize errors, reduce software vulnerabilities, and provide guidance to developers on how to remediate discovered vulnerabilities.

- Work with the information technology industry and others to apply concepts from the Trusted Computing Initiative from the Trusted Computing Group (**https://www.trustedcomputinggroup.org/home**) to build and protect a core "Trusted Financial Service Processing Layer" upon which our applications can safely be built, and upon which the financial industry can rely on to provide a continuous level of financial services at some minimum essential level in the face of massive failure, attack, or successful fraud.

- Develop a standardized methodology for designing, implementing, testing, and measuring application software to be less vulnerable to attack. Such a methodology should include the ability to accurately measure and forecast the security of application code.

- Educate software developers on secure development techniques because better coding practices are needed to reduce the number of software flaws in the long term.

Potential Research Projects

Research to support this challenge is needed to:

- Develop cost effective design principles for secure application designs that can reliably rank and distinguish the relative levels of security of different software products.

- Develop tools for developing, measuring, and testing secure software to a higher degree of accuracy.

- Develop strategies and tools for making/transforming existing or legacy software applications to a more secure state by adding layers of protection.

- Anticipate and predict future software attacks, exploits that could detect known vulnerabilities, and variance to known vulnerabilities via simulation models in order to better anticipate threats. Simulation models include tabletop games and computer modeling.

- Allocate more equitable liability for software vulnerabilities to create better incentives for responsible parties to implement appropriate controls including testing, user training, and standard configuration.

- Develop effective procurement standards, software developer education, and testing guidelines.

- Design diversity and resilience in software to make it more robust and resistant to attack.

- Understand the interaction of software and their vulnerabilities.

- Develop a standard for secure software development (e.g., review and revamp of ISO/IEC 12207 and linkage to ISO 17799) that integrates security requirements and principles in each phase of the software development life cycle.

- Develop a standard for software procurement (to mitigate adhesion contracts) that clearly establishes the security requirements for custom-developed software, COTS, and embedded (including network devices) software.

- Develop tools (e.g., IDE plug-in, etc.) to automatically scan and enforce security principles based on a centralized policy server as the software is being coded. This tool should also provide and enforce the use of security API (similar to OWASP ESAPI) for common validation routines.

- Develop a methodology and tools to evaluate software security within short timeframes, and in an economically efficient manner by considering real-life deployment/usage scenarios. Also develop accompanying star ratings (1 through 5) that are easily understandable by a purchaser.

- Make the Common Criteria commercially viable for research efforts in developing and validating already-developed evaluation criteria that is meaningful for the Banking and Finance Sector.

- Develop a "self-healing" framework and utilities that would automatically adapt to defend against the potential exploits of code vulnerabilities or security weaknesses of underlying services.

- Research the application of Six Sigma, CMM, and other quality-enhancing practices to software development.

Challenge 2: More Secure and Resilient Financial Transaction Systems

The Situation

The Banking and Finance Sector relies on an information technology infrastructure, including computing hardware, software, and telecommunications networks. Some of this infrastructure is owned and operated by financial institutions and some is provided by third party service providers in the US and around the globe. This infrastructure is probed and attacked by a variety of adversaries, including criminal elements and nation-states. These adversaries exploit vulnerabilities in people, processes, and technologies and perpetrate attacks for financial gain, to steal proprietary information, or to undermine consumer confidence in the financial services industry and US economy. Threats from adversaries are increasing, raising concerns over the integrity of devices, networks, and applications. The infrastructure is also vulnerable to natural disasters, pandemics, and other outages. Although the financial services, information technology, and telecommunications industries have responded to these challenges with initiatives to address security, integrity, and resilience, significant risks remain in terms of security breaches, fraud (including identity theft), service disruptions, and data integrity.

The key to maintaining the integrity of the financial services industry is more secure and resilient financial transaction systems. It must resist interception and tampering over an increasingly vulnerable environment in which the trustworthiness of networks and devices is uncertain. One facet is ensuring that networks and devices are "clean" when restoring service after an interruption. Reconstitution of data after an attack requires an additional step: decontamination, which is the process of distinguishing a clean system state (unaffected by the intruder) from the portions of infected system state, and eliminating the causes of those differences. Because system users would prefer as little good data as possible be discarded, this problem is quite difficult. Also of primary importance is the retention and reconstruction of transaction history while simultaneously being fully engaged in business continuity operations and executing a recovery plan. Other sectors have expressed concerns about extending their continuity plans to include vital information found on remote workstations. The possibility of this dislocation of normal corporate boundaries could be strained when relying on a distributed computing model.

Remote access is necessary for enhancing productivity and as a tool for business continuity planning purposes. For example, financial institutions have developed business continuity plans to ensure employees can access networks if core facilities are not available. The most significant outcome of the FSSCC/FBIIC pandemic planning exercise in 2007 was the heavy reliance by multiple industries on the Internet as the backup communication channel to support business continuity. Use of company-owned devices in conjunction with personally-owned devices introduces serious security challenges. Issues arise regarding the downloading, printing, and storage of sensitive customer and company information; potential data loss as a result of theft of mobile and personally-owned devices; introduction of malicious code into the corporate network from the personally-owned devices or company devices that are not managed as strongly as desktop systems; remote support issues; compliance with regulatory requirements; and the ability to reroute phone calls and faxes, etc.

The challenge is in finding the right mix of hardware and software that gives employees the ability to conduct their work off-site while still adhering to all of the controls and monitoring afforded by corporate facilities, and without introducing the company and the data to excessive incremental risk. It should also provide employees the ability to seamlessly move from one location to another while retaining their "session state" and desktop customization.

Impact and Consequences

The impact and consequences of attacks or operational failures on the transactions could cause serious service disruptions to customers resulting in losses, liquidity problems, and lack of market and consumer confidence due to concerns about data integrity. This could lead to severe market disruptions, economic disruptions, and public panic. Also, credible threats of service disruptions could lead to situations where adversaries could blackmail, extort, or coerce financial institutions in ways that could be detrimental to individual firms and the overall economy.

Desired Functionality

2a More secure and resilient financial transaction systems that enable transacting parties (e.g., between financial institutions, and between institutions and customers) to securely exchange financial information and commands (e.g. account information, payment instructions, etc.) with confidence even though the message protocol traverses untrustworthy communications networks and computing nodes. The protocols should:

2a.1 Reliably and unambiguously identify the originator of a message.

2a.2 Ensure only the intended recipient(s) is able to receive and understand the message

2a.3 Protect message content against tampering and identify any attempt to modify message content.

2a.4 Promote interoperability among financial institutions by use of existing or enhanced industry standards to encode and encrypt message content.

2a.5 Support use as a service among diverse financial service applications.

2a.6 Scale to support very high transaction rates, on a scale exceeding hundreds of millions of transactions per day, operating globally, 24x7.

2a.7 Motivate migration to more secure protocols and tamper proof records.

2a.8 Anticipate threat evolution and evolve ahead of them (e.g., flexible responses to chameleon automated attacks introduced by organized crime, technology that would provide a tamper-proof record of document access for auditing / monitoring multiple secure email systems).

2b The architecture of a more secure, more resilient, and more flexible financial transaction system infrastructure should:

2b.1 Address secure data replication in large quantities across great distances.

2b.2 Shift load from congested or compromised facilities to other available facilities with care not to create a data replication issue.

2b.3 Provision public networks or endpoints (i.e. banks) to dedicate secure bandwidth to financial services transactions.

2b.4 Support the creation of shared capacity able to absorb demand displaced by a wide variety of incidents (e.g., pandemic requiring massive work-from-home scenario), and engineer a protected service that would give priority access when there is congestion.

2b.5 Extend connectivity to areas in which basic services are unavailable using local power generation, rapid deployment of wireless communications, mobile kiosks, or other innovative techniques.

2b.6 Leverage the economic efficiency provided by public communications networks and commercial off-the-shelf (COTS) computer systems.

2b.7 Provide sufficient redundancy and flexibility to continue operation without significant degradation of services while under cyber and physical attack, or during natural disasters.

2b.8 Reduce dependencies on the critical infrastructure provided by other industries.

2c Develop more resilience for the communications and processing capabilities required by the financial industry, and define alternative communications channels that are less reliant on any particular Internet connectivity channel:

2c.1 Prioritize in favor of commercial and critical telecommunication traffic from casual and critical use to improve quality of service and maintain resilience.

2c.2 Increase resilience of connectivity between continents and countries (e.g., Internet cable cuts).

2c.3 Provide incentives to business partners to meet the necessary security and resilience needs of the Banking and Finance Sector.

2c.4 ROI for more secure protocols.

2c.5 Provide secure hardware and software that can connect securely to the customer without relying on their ability to configure devices.

2c.6 Apply top level domain or high assurance certificates that can be used for priority handling.

2c.7 Improve rapidly deployable emergency communications.

2c.8 Prioritization by addresses versus content.

2d Enhance the protections available to prevent the increasingly common downloads of malware created by criminal elements (i.e., "crimeware") that bypass existing PC defenses such as anti-virus and anti-spyware. The criminal element uses crimeware, among other things, to capture consumer information (e.g., via the "Silent Banker" malware) or use the end user's PC as a node in a botnet.

2e Improve the level of defenses available to prevent malicious downloads of software.

2f Minimize the amount of proactive interaction required by users, particularly consumer-type users utilizing home-based PCs, to protect their computers against crimeware.

2g Develop a platform-independent transaction system that maintains adequate integrity even when an endpoint is compromised.

2g.1 Ensure that transactions are delivered to the bank exactly as entered by the customer, without change, addition, or deletion.

2g.2 Maintain the customers' ability to transact business using any platform other than that of their choice.

2g.3 The transactional system should be independent of any specific platform.

Potential Research Projects

Research to support this challenge is needed to:

• Better understand the changing threats and develop strategies to adapt to them.

• Design better protocols that can operate with un-trusted devices and vulnerabilities in software and hardware.

• Develop metrics to evaluate the resilience of an enterprise in a way that permits continuous improvement.

• Reduce the cost and improve the usability of industry standard cryptographic solutions.

- Explore the application of advanced encryption such as quantum cryptography and steganographic[30] techniques to the secure and resilient transaction system problem.

- Improve the underlying trust models by developing novel processes and technologies.

- Develop tools, in the form of simulation models, for the system and network infrastructure as well as for information and transaction processing. Such models will enable financial institutions to evaluate the impact of incidents and develop contingency and response plans if attacks, natural disasters, or other events were to disrupt the flow of information and transactions.

- Use integrated multi-channel transaction protocols to enhance diversity and resilience.

- Identify feasible alternatives to the current financial transaction systems.

- Analyze how a top level domain (TLD) for the banking and finance sector could enhance resilience and mutual authentication. For example, the Internet Corporation for Assigned Names and Numbers (ICANN) offers a means whereby key sectors can establish criteria for a TLD. Research is needed to understand how such means would address the security concerns of the financial services industry, what ground rules would need to be established, and what the potential benefits might be in terms of enhanced security and reduced fraud. This includes whether a sector-specific TLD would be a marketing differentiator and thus worth the investment beyond the security and fraud savings. Further research is necessary to understand the following: (a) assurance levels of parties; (b) how to treat financial institutions and service providers on a global basis; (c) consumer education; (d) transition costs; (e) impact to brand and marketing; and (f) impact on reducing denial of service attacks on individual financial institutions and the entire sector.

- Analyze how data tagging and application security could enable computing in environments where the trustworthiness of networks and devices is questionable (in conjunction with challenge #5 on "data centric protection strategies").

- Identify mechanisms for more effective automatic network load shifting.

- Research approaches for a system to adapt around disruptions, including shifting operation to a minimum essential mode that allows the continuation of critical services in the face of reduced capacity, communications, and resources.

- Create new decontamination approaches for discarding as little good data as possible, and for removing active and potential infections, on a system that cannot be shut down for decontamination.

- Research alternative organizational and operational modes that can allow the operation of loosely coupled, decentralized locations with minimum connectivity and communications.

- Improve communication protocols that could free additional bandwidth or allow bandwidth switching during a crisis.

- Develop strategies to overcome vulnerabilities of transcontinental cables and route diversity constraints.

- Develop strategies to identify, segregate and route traffic based on bandwidth requirements of applications.

- Research capabilities to use low bandwidth mobile devices as alternatives.

- Understand minimum, essential financial operational procedures and processes that are capable of operating with minimal survivable communications and processing capacity.

- Understand how desktop virtualization, suspend/resume processing, message compression algorithms, transmission optimization for performance enhancement and capacity optimization, validation of software components, both local and remote, data integrity, etc. can enhance security and resilience.

- Research self-executing (i.e., require little to no interaction with PC users to operate), commercially reasonable mechanisms that improve on currently available PC defenses to prevent the download of crimeware.

---

[30] Steganography is the art and science of writing hidden messages in such a way that no one apart from the sender and intended recipient even realizes there is a hidden message. By contrast, cryptography obscures the meaning of a message, but it does not conceal the fact that there is a message. (Wikipedia)

Challenge 3: Enrollment and Identity Credential Management

The Situation

A secure financial infrastructure requires reliable and unambiguous identification of all parties involved in a transaction and non-repudiation of authorized transactions. Current technologies offer "spot" solutions that secure an aspect of identity management; however, many vulnerabilities remain. Although strong authentication credentialing technology exists, the initial identification of and linkage to an individual's identity to an authentication credential and the need to replace lost or stolen credentials remain weak links. Financial institutions rely on the individual's possession of knowledge that can be stolen, or by biometrics that can be spoofed, and may not scale up to millions of individuals without sacrificing performance. Moreover, the lack of strong mutual authentication allows for, among other things, the ability for the launching of successful man-in-the-middle attacks.[31] Financial institutions typically rely on "spot" authentication in which the financial institution authenticates customers before a transaction. Research is needed to develop more continuous authentication and credentialing.

Impact and Consequences

There are widely varying estimates of losses due to identity-based financial fraud. A public perception of widespread risk of identity-based financial fraud has led to declining consumer confidence in online financial services, further resulting in a loss of potential customer adoption. This perception could also increase the risk of new laws, regulations, and supervisory requirements that yield sub-optimal solutions and new compliance costs without tangible results in terms of reduced losses and higher customer satisfaction. The absence of agreed-upon architectural solutions, and strong, affordable, well-accepted, easy to use identification and mutual authentication means that vulnerabilities will persist, especially as criminal elements perpetrate financial fraud through attacks on identity management systems.

Desired Functionality

Define the architecture of an 'identity layer' suitable for incorporation in all financial services protocols and communications. This identity layer should:

• Provide secure and reliable identification of all parties.

• Provide strong mutual authentication of all parties using existing authentication methods such as biometrics or new methods to be developed that minimize customer inconvenience, are well-accepted, and minimize personal intrusion and interaction.

---

[31] In cryptography, the man-in-the-middle, or bucket-brigade, attack (often abbreviated MITM) is a form of active eavesdropping in which the attacker makes independent connections with the victims and relays messages between them, making them believe that they are talking directly to each other over a private connection, when in fact the entire conversation is controlled by the attacker. The attacker must be able to intercept all messages going between the two victims and inject new ones, which is straightforward in many circumstances (for example, the owner of a public wireless access point can, in principle, conduct MITM attacks on the users). A man-in-the-middle attack can only be successful when the attacker can impersonate each endpoint to the satisfaction of the other. Most cryptographic protocols include some form of endpoint authentication specifically to prevent MITM attacks. For example, SSL authenticates the server using a mutually trusted certification authority. (Wikipedia)

- Provide a reasonable level of non-repudiation of financial transactions undertaken by authenticated participants.

- Preserve identity across all interfaces and protocols.

- Develop a capability for continuous authentication throughout the entire transaction interaction.

- Include procedures that verify an applicant's right to enroll under a particular identity.

- Support new approaches to strengthening enrollment procedures, including new knowledge-based identification approaches, and investigating and developing new, stronger approaches to identity verification, including the use of biometrics.

- Provide flexibility to incorporate improved methods for an individual or enterprise who has verified identity with a financial institution to use that identity in dealings with other institutions – financial or non-financial – including 'trust models' that address liability issues.

- Improve the scalability of any solution and issues related to preserving end-to-end identity management in systems comprising many subsystems.

Potential Research Projects

Research to support this challenge is needed to:

- Integrate national security-based identification standards (e.g., REAL ID) into mature and robust access control technology.

- Protect the privacy and confidentiality of identity data and identity management artifacts, such as enrollment questions, throughout the identity management domain.

- Incorporate appropriate privacy and confidentiality protections into the identity management process.

- Understand the social and psychological issues that affect whether a solution is acceptable to the public, including the factors that make a security procedure "feel" intrusive versus reassuring to the public, and methods to present security enhancements in a way that enhances public confidence without causing resentment.

- Document risks inherent in advances in identity management and methods of mitigating and managing these risks.

- Quantify current vulnerabilities and losses and the effect of solutions in eliminating or reducing these risks.

- Develop a framework with more precise terminology to better understand the nature of Identity Management and the distinctions between identification, verification, authentication, and authorization, including a more fine-grained approach to establishing and managing identity claims and authorizations.

- Understand how to implement cost effective and customer-accepted authentication and identification technologies, such as continuous physiological and biometric indicators.

- Test the effectiveness of technologies that protect consumers against social engineering attacks such as phishing, vishing, or smsing.

- Apply novel methods of zero-knowledge challenges and continuous authentication monitoring.

- Apply advanced behavioral monitoring, including anomaly pattern detection integrated with physiological monitoring.

- Research methods to integrate effective methods of multi-channel authentication.

Challenge 4: Understanding the Human Insider Threat

The Situation

Financial institutions grant access to confidential information to authorized parties. To establish and maintain trust in this access granting process, financial institutions use a variety of tools and controls to identify, verify, authenticate, and authorize trustworthy individuals and contractors. Measures include background checks, credit history checks, and other historical data checks. The insider threat problem is a particularly difficult because of the interplay between technical, legal, managerial, and ethical issues. Financial institutions recognize that current measures provide only a "coarse-grained" screening for obvious human threats to begin the access granting process; individuals are granted access to networks, systems, databases, applications, and ultimately customer and business information based on their job or role in the institution. The process is enforced via a highly complex set of overlapping operational and technical controls, which requires that a large percentage of each financial institution's total information protection budget is dedicated to access management, control, and reporting.

Despite the pre-employment/engagement checking processes, and the layering of costly operational and technical controls, financial institutions continue to experience damage from the unprofessional, malicious, or criminal activities committed by individuals with authorized access, sometimes in coordination with external individuals, criminal organizations, or terrorists. Current approaches suggest adding additional layers – technological or procedural – of surveillance processes to detect, identify, and help stop the unwanted activities of authorized individuals. However, such approaches, while they may reduce undesirable activities, add substantial operating costs to an already costly access management approach.

Financial institutions currently have tools that could be useful in determining improper behavior of insiders. Many of these tools are based on physical and logical access but are typically not integrated. Improvements in security information management are needed to detect and prevent improper insider behavior. A critical component of improving security information management is ensuring that appropriate controls are in place to address privacy and other human resource protections.

Impact and Consequences

Events where authorized access has been exploited within individual financial institutions can damage the reputation of the institution and, taken as a group, can degrade customer confidence in the entire financial infrastructure. Continued problems could cause a downward confidence spiral in which internal attacks could become increasingly effective at reducing customer confidence. The human threats problem appears to be growing despite increased funding and oversight within financial institutions and from financial regulators. While most attacks by insiders are for financial gain, there is concern of a potential terrorist threat to the national financial infrastructure from coordinated insider attacks by individuals with access to multiple institutions.

Desired Functionality

Bring together a research team with wide ranging skill sets to accurately and thoroughly identify, measure, and document personal/behavioral, operating process/procedural, technical/technological policies and the financial aspects of this problem. The research should:

- Review the scope of operating issues faced by individual financial institutions, including defining the problem in terms of a coordinated attack on the National Financial Infrastructure.

- Provide a framework for describing and understanding the totality of the human threat, and produce or advance a common language for describing the problem in its various forms.

- Provide conclusions about the nature, scope, size, extent, and direction of movement so that financial institutions' decision-makers can understand their place in the problem on both an individual and national basis.

- Describe a set of workable tactical solutions that could be implemented individually by financial institutions to decrease the risk of threats from an authorized user.

- Investigate technologies such as behavioral modeling and social network analysis, as well as advanced methodologies for sharing the results.

- Track and provide auditable records of what subsequent actions were taken and by whom.

- Investigate application of sensors for monitoring and surveillance of, for example, critical financial and banking center operations. Sensors can control doors, tag computers, and operate cameras and other monitoring devices to provide security information remotely.

Potential Research Projects

Research to support this challenge is needed to:

- Develop a holistic approach for authorizing insiders at all phases of the authorization lifecycle, given that threats can change faster than layers of control and surveillance can be added in response.

- Develop data to frame the likelihood of the insider threat.

- Identify tactical solutions for identifying and responding to the human threat that automatically terminates access rights, including (but not limited to) behavior and physiological modeling; better means of continuous psychological and background testing that is more predictive; application of social network analysis; effective sensor techniques for monitoring behavior; and monitoring technologies to detect when a trusted insider is doing something that is deemed a threat to the institution.

- Balance privacy rights with identity mechanisms.

- Measure the effectiveness of new approaches to reducing incidents and the likelihood of human insider fraud.

- Improve the automated aspects of audit log review and activities.

- Develop an incentive structure to help manage the threat.

- Measure the effectiveness of new approaches to reducing the number of incidents and the likelihood of insider fraud. Thereafter, use the usual audit rule; the set up changes should require more than one person.

Challenge 5: Data Centric Protection Strategies

The Situation

Even if the financial services industry builds a more secure and resilient infrastructure to protect financial transactions (as addressed in Challenge #2), it is still vulnerable to having sensitive information stolen by criminal elements and other adversaries who attack less secure systems outside the financial services industries' secure transaction infrastructure with whom we share portions of this information (e.g., merchants and third party vendors). Preserving the integrity of each transaction involves identification, authentication, and authorization of each transaction to ensure that counterparties are not criminals or money-launderers, and that sensitive information is protected and its loss, copying, or tampering is detected. While financial institutions have tools that protect data while it resides in a certain environment, these tools are not effective when the data is taken out of that controlled environment (e.g., when a user cuts and pastes in another form). A key challenge is focusing on metadata to understand when data is accessed, updated, or copied.

Impact and Consequences

The result of these trends, if not checked, would be for customers to lose confidence in the banking system, which has become increasingly dependent on these computer networks and systems. If this situation is not addressed, the banking and financial services industry will face critical brand erosion and significant loss of customers, as well as financial losses realized by both their customers and themselves. Increasing incidents of privacy breaches will lead to a loss of consumer confidence in online financial services. Theft of sensitive data can also provide the information needed to launch more successful denial-of-service attacks.

Desired Functionality

5   Define the architecture of a financial information system that provides a comprehensive privacy and security model. Such a system should:

  5.1   Provide strong access, authentication, and entitlement controls.

  5.2   Provide a means or mechanism (e.g., "tagged" data elements or metadata stored in a data dictionary) that enables a rules-based model where data protection, based on established control requirements, is automatically enforced by the infrastructure to prevent unauthorized access or modification while preserving the principles of Discretionary Access Controls.

  5.3   Track information across its entire life-cycle, requiring institutions to:

    5.3.1 Track and provide auditable records of who accessed what information and when.

    5.3.2 Track and provide auditable records of how the information was used and what actions were taken.

5.3.3 Track and provide auditable records indicating whether the information or derivatives of this information were shared, with whom it was shared, when, and where.

5.3.4 Track and provide auditable records of what subsequent actions were taken and by whom.

5.3.5 Determine how to detect when data has been tampered with.

5.4 Explore how to develop data dictionaries in which transactions that identify data are classified and encrypted.

5.5 Provide alerts and the ability to set and enforce unified data-centric policies to prohibit and constrain attempts at using or sharing information in ways that violate policies established for the data.

5.6 Provide warning indicators when usage and access is not normal.

5.7 Accommodate remote access of enterprise information and processing resources.

5.8 Accommodate personally-owned devices used by employees and contractors.

5.9 Address the security implications of Web 2.0.

5.10 Increase scale to economically support hundreds of billions of records.

5.11 Interoperate with a system that makes information securely accessible across untrustworthy communications networks and computing nodes (see Challenge #1).

5.12 Provide advanced analytics and simulation tools for accurate fraud and attack forecasting.

Potential Research Projects

Research to support this challenge is needed to:

- Develop secure data file and document tagging technologies that provide audit trails of access.

- Develop effective digital data tagging technologies that provide for enforcement of access/authentication and authorization rules across any application or access point used to access the information.

- Develop standards and best practices to classify and tag data.

- Develop enforcement requirements for compliance with data classification practices.

- Automate processes where multiple parties provide data and control decision points.

- Preserve accountability through data ownership and control.

- Investigate feasibility of "rights management" technology as a means of enforcing policies governing access to information and how it is used, as well as providing alerts when violations are attempted or detected.

- Allocate more equitable liability for software vulnerabilities to create better incentives for responsible parties to implement appropriate controls including testing, user training, and standard configuration.

Challenge 6: Better Measures of the Value of Security Investments

The Situation

The financial industry seeks research on the life-cycle costs of security technologies that support critical infrastructure protection, and the creation of cost-benefit models that can be adopted within institutions and across the industry. One of the key issues in the adoption of improved protective technologies and processes is the ability of the purchasing organizations to fully understand the costs and benefits of security technologies. Information protection organizations, as part of their regular business, can effectively evaluate specific cost elements for various protective programs in terms of operating cost, contracting costs, and the cost of purchasing the needed technology for an organization. However, information protection organizations typically do not have good estimates of the total lifecycle costs of the protective programs on the business lines that are asked to implement, own, and manage these protective programs over the long-term. Across the entire Banking and Finance Sector, the information protection and risk management community is generally not well-equipped to accurately or completely define, estimate, calculate, measure, or communicate the benefits that result from protective programs. Further exacerbating this issue is that the "benefits" of security are often intangible and often relate more to loss avoidance, making traditional return-on-investment (ROI) calculations difficult. There needs to be a stronger correlation between security investment and the reduction of risk and subsequent loss. Some methods used today to justify security investments may not align or be equivalent with methodologies under Generally Accepted Accounting Principles (GAAP). Research is needed to establish a baseline risk and to understand changes from the baseline that result from investment. This research also could benefit the broader risk management community.

Impact and Consequences

The Sector continues to focus on security processes rather than security outcomes, and as a result, there is scant knowledge of which security investments and practices have an effect on security outcomes. A clear and accepted methodology to accurately measure both costs and benefits would speed the deployment of improved security technologies within organizations and across the Industry. There is a need for a disciplined approach based on clear outcome definitions combined with a causality oriented learning and improvement feedback loop; a standard language and financially certifiable methodology to define, estimate, measure, and communicate costs and benefits would assist all institutions. The sooner the industry adopts a standard cost-to-benefit approach, the more rapidly information protection will be integrated into financial institutions' priorities.

Desired Functionality

Develop a standardized methodology for calculating ROI for critical infrastructure protection (CIP) and security technology that is relevant to the financial industry. Such a methodology should:

- Develop cost-benefit models describing the costs and benefits of improved CIP and security technology. The output of this research should result in agreement from participating institutions and the industry at large for adoption of these models and approaches. This model should include data that are appropriate to estimate the total lifecycle cost when implementing individual information protection programs, and form a repository for case studies that may be accessed and used by other institutions.

- Develop common mathematics and rules for estimating program deployment costs that both allow Institutions to "plug-in" their specific costs, and are open to varied implementation approaches.

- Quantify the costs/benefits for information protection as mandated by the Sarbanes-Oxley and Gramm-Leach-Bliley Acts, and link to an overall approach to provide reporting to meet SOX, GLBA, and other legal and regulatory requirements.

- Establish commonly acceptable cost-to-benefit estimation, measurement, and communication processes and methods for the financial industry.

- Focus on security outcomes rather than security processes to determine what security investments and practices have an effect on security outcomes.

Potential Research Projects

Research to support this challenge is needed to:

- Identify financial modeling methodologies that:
  - Quantify the costs and direct and indirect benefits of security software,
  - Are sufficiently close to existing ROI models as to be understood easily by financial institutions' senior and executive management, and
  - Are sufficiently consistent with existing accounting principles to be both acceptable to and understood by FI's financial staffs.

- Develop tools to better understand the cost-benefit trade-offs and methods to quantify levels of investment and set priorities.

Challenge 7: Development of Practical Standards

The Situation

One of the prevailing techniques for closing the gap between state-of-the-art and state-of-the-practice is the development of practical standards and suggested practices. In an attempt to further the protection of the banking and finance critical infrastructures, numerous documents outlining suggested practices have been developed, most addressing a closely circumscribed segment of banking and finance systems and practices. Standards such as COBIT, ISO 27002, PCI-DSS, and the NIST Special Publications 800 series are in development or have been issued. While efforts to promulgate these documents and encourage adoption of these standards have been uneven, this challenge continues to consistently score near the top whenever these R&D opportunities are prioritized. Part of the problem is that, to date, the industry has been unable to quantitatively correlate best practices with reduced risk. If such a relationship could be determined and quantified, financial institutions would have the tools needed to justify risk management and risk reduction measures. This analysis could, in turn, assist the industry in agreeing on a common and consistent set of practices. A related question is how practitioners and regulators should adopt or consider these in developing robust and resilient infrastructures vis-à-vis the confusion caused by so many different best practices guides and standards.

Impact and Consequences

It typically takes a long period of time and involves a lot of costly trial and error to develop best practices in response to changing regulatory requirements. This process is inefficient and costly to financial institutions as well as to the regulators. Inaccessible or uncoordinated standards and best practices, and unclear return on investment (ROI) measurements, contribute to the gap between state-of-the-art and state-of-the-practice. In this space there are many chronically missed opportunities and the potential for substantial gains based on a modest investment.

Desired Functionality

Create a practical standards repository and incident database available for members of the Banking and Finance Sector to enable research into the effectiveness and correlation of effective practices that improve risk management. Industry, enterprise, system, and process practices and standards should be sought out, summarized, categorized, indexed, and made available to the community. The Department of Justice standards registry is an example of this (**http://it.ojp.gov/jsr/public/index.jsp**). Such a repository could include the following:

- A database for use by academicians through which they can develop a correlation of existing standards, the risks each correlated set of standards addresses, the level of protection, and limits to protection each correlated set of standards provides.

- Standards for integrating physical and logical security systems.

- Standards across network connections that ensure security across wired and wireless devices with particular concern to interoperability and privacy.

- Voice and video conferencing for VOIP over data networks.

- Standards for access control.

- Standards for outsourcing critical functions, particularly those related to networks and information systems, that address the implications for cyber security, business continuity, and overall risk management.

- Standards for business continuity planning, including methods for determining the minimal operational requirements of an organization, strategies for achieving these requirements after a contingency event, selecting recovery time objectives (RTO) and recovery point objectives (RPO) for data replication, considering the distance between operational locations, the nature of critical business processes, cost, and sound business practices.

- Standards regarding the ability of key components of the Banking and Finance Sector to establish and maintain communication between their various primary and alternate facilities with the capability to conduct transactions at a sufficient volume and level of accuracy.

- Practices regarding the verification and preservation of physical diversity of telecommunications routing

- Practices in code development.

- Identification of the key elements of secure software code/products.

- Quantifying the impact of "safe practices" on reducing exposure.

- Practices of shared responsibilities that lead to better security controls.

- Practices in data replication that increase resilience by seamlessly providing redundant services and processing capabilities across multiple operations centers.

This endeavor should also investigate new, innovative technologies that might improve the current state of best practices.

Potential Research Projects

Research to support this challenge is needed to:

- Correlate the impact of standards and practices on the actual state of security.

- Review laws and regulations (e.g., Bank Secrecy Act, Gramm-Leach-Bliley, Sarbanes-Oxley) and analyze the period of time it took to develop a standardized best practices approach within the industry to implement the new regulations.

- Develop approaches that would be more cost-effective and efficient for financial institutions to comply with requirements.

- Build models of disaster situations and then play interactive tabletop game to simulate various scenarios.

Appendix A: Members of the FSSCC R&D Committee

C. Warren Axelrod, Financial Services Technology Consortium

Andy Bach, Securities Industry Automation Corporation

John Carlson, BITS/Financial Services Roundtable (Chairman)

Frank Castelluccio, The Options Clearing Corporation

Dan DeWaal, The Options Clearing Corporation

Eric Guerrino, Bank of New York Mellon Corporation

Mark Merkow, American Express Company

William Nelson, Financial Services Information Sharing and Analysis Center

Dan Schutzer, Financial Services Technology Consortium

Public Sector Representatives: Brian Peretti, U.S. Department of the Treasury

In addition to the above R&D Committee members, Paul Smocer, Ann Patterson, Matt Ribe and Ryan Waggoner of BITS/ Financial Services Roundtable provided substantive comments and edits on this draft of the report. Jennifer Bayuk, formerly with Bear Stearns & Co, served as the chair of the R&D Committee from 2006 until February 2008 and contributed to the development of this paper.

www.ingramcontent.com/pod-product-compliance
Lightning Source LLC
Chambersburg PA
CBHW080316290526
45790CB00005B/2061